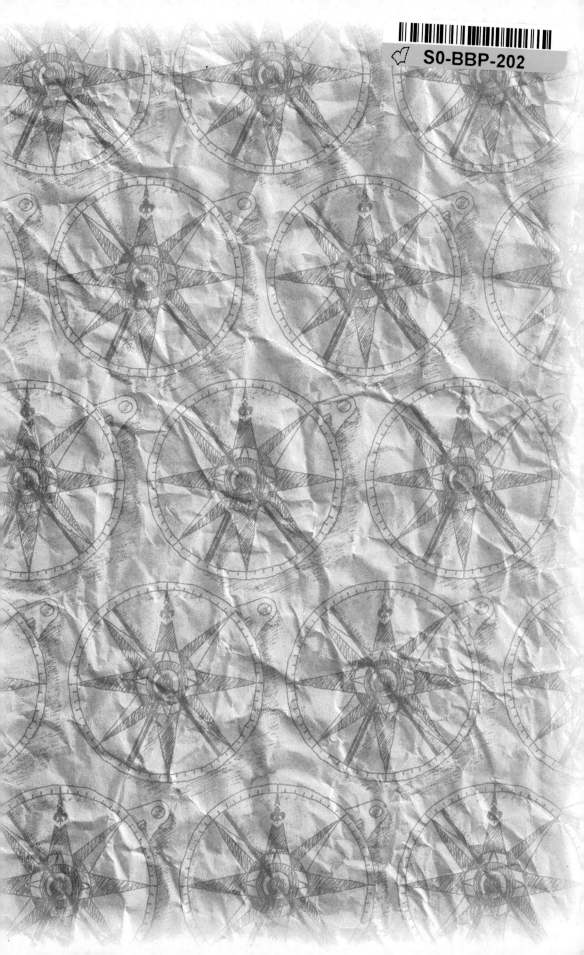

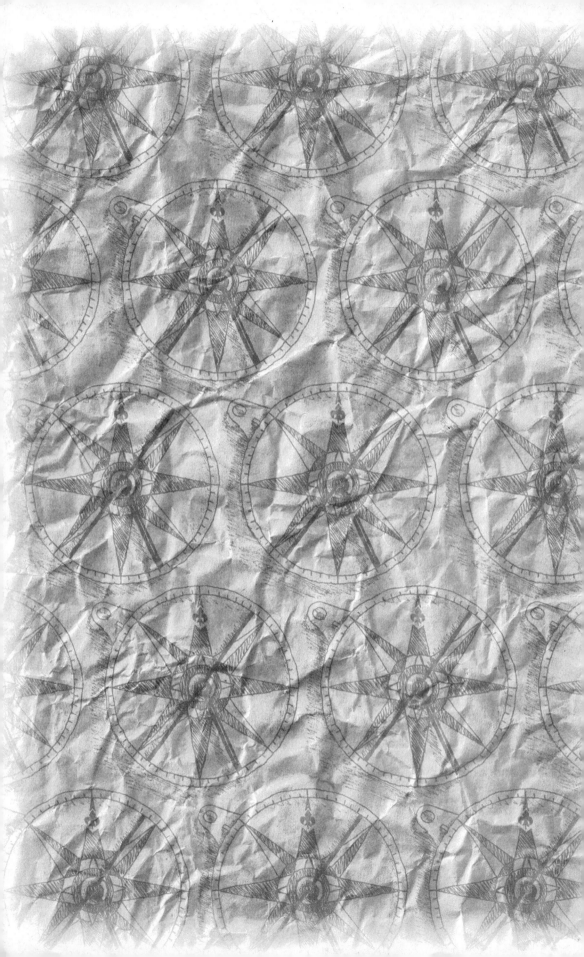

A Scout Leader's Guide to Youth Leadership Training

Working the Patrol Method

by

Eagle Scouts Rob Faris, Ted Knight & Harry Wimbrough

Illustrated by Eagle Scout Joseph Durel

ISBN 978-0-945253-20-4

Published in the United States of America by Thornsbury Bailey & Brown, Inc.

Printed in Canada by Webcom

Dedication

We dedicate this book to the memory of Robert Stephenson Smyth Baden-Powell, Lord of Gilwell, Chief Scout of the World — and to all Scouts and Scouters he inspired to carry on his work in the greatest, most successful youth program in the history of the world. We also dedicate this book to our Scoutmasters, Assistant Scoutmasters and other leaders including our Patrol Leaders and our Senior Patrol Leaders. They led and taught us when we were Scouts. Through their example, they have kept Baden-Powell's campfires of Scouting burning brightly for us and many other Scouts. We thank them for the gift of Scouting. We further dedicate this book to the worldwide brotherhood of Scouting. Scouting means different things to different people around the world, but the essentials are universal. We also dedicate this book to our sons and to the Scouts of Troop 624 Arlington, Virginia, who have inspired us by making Scouting their own and challenging us to be the best Scout Leaders we can be.

Inspiration

This book was several years in the making. Initial inspiration came from the following email:

Hi Ted,

Just saying hi and updating you on what is going on down here. I am still stationed at Fort Hood in Texas. I am a battle captain for a signal battalion down here, but still just a 1st LT. I deployed to the Middle East last October when we started bombing Afghanistan. It seems funny but I have used all of the skills I learned in Boy Scouts all of the time through the last 6 yrs in the Army. At times, it has given me quite an advantage and of course, it is a great comfort to have such a repository of experience and knowledge to use toward tactical advantage when you have 60 guys' lives on the line. Thank you to you and all of the Scout leaders who taught me these skills and set me on the path of being a good leader.

Sincerely,

Bryson Bort
First Lieutenant, United States Army
Troop 624 Eagle Scout Class of 1996

Contents

Foreword 9

Introduction 13
We Are Often Distracted from Effective
Scout Leadership Training and Mentoring 13

   It Takes Discipline and Focus to Be Effective 13
   A Scout Troop Is the Perfect Place to Mold and Mentor Leaders 14
   Leadership Training and Mentoring Is Hands-On, Not Theoretical 14
   The Patrol Method Is the Recipe for Scout Leadership Training 15
   Many Scouts Will Not Lead Without Encouragement
     from Their Scoutmasters. 15
   Are You Prepared to Train and Mentor Tomorrow's Leaders? 16
   The Best Scoutmasters Are Stage Directors 16
   How This Guide Is Organized 17

Section 1
Understanding and Telling "The Why" 21

   Leadership Is Based on Trust 24
   Telling "The Why" Helps Build Trust. 24
   Clear Rational Thinking and Communication. 25
   Teaching Moments 27
   Telling "The Why" Is Important 28

Section 2
"The Why" of Scout Leadership Training
(The True Yarn of Baden-Powell on Brownsea Island) 33

   The Game with a Purpose 33
   The Inception of Scouting's Outdoor Program. 34
   Giving Boys Important Responsibilities and Uniforms 35
   Baden-Powell's Great Experiment on Brownsea Island 36
   Scouting Caught on in the USA and All Over the World. 42

Section 3

The Patrol Method: A Scoutmaster's Perspective 47

What Is the Patrol Method? 48
The Patrol Method Defined 50
Give Your Patrol Leaders Real Authority 51
The Power, Privilege and Responsibility of Self-Governance.............. 53
The Patrol Leader's Pledge 59
Patrol Member Rights and Responsibilities 60

Section 4

Patrol Method: Building the Team 61

The Magic of Patrol Teamwork and Patrol Spirit 62
The Patrol Leader's Work and Authority 64
Forming the Patrol 66
Patrol Identity.. 68
Leading the Individual: Learning about Each Patrol Member 70
Understand the Characteristics
    and Needs of Your Team and Each Team Member...................... 70
Know and Use Your Team Resources 72
Control Undesirable Behavior 74
Motivational Leadership.. 75
Scouting Is Not "Pass/Fail" 76
Control Team Performance 79

Section 5

Striving for Excellence: Doing Your Best 81

Section 6

Caring Leadership 87

Historical Perspective... 88
Ethics and Caring in Developing Servant Leadership 90
Ethics from the Top Down: Setting the Example 91
Instilling Strong Values... 93
The Patrol Method Misapplied.. 94
Training Leaders to Care about the Entire Group 96
Managing Cliques.. 97

Section 7
Planning: How to Facilitate Without Taking Over 99

Getting Scouts To Visualize a Plan 104
What Do You Write Down? 105
Patrol Activity Planner 107
Troop Annual Meeting 108
Troop Monthly Planner 111
Troop Meeting Planner 112
Scouting Is Fun! 113

Section 8
Shared Leadership 115

Don't Be "Mr. Do-It-All" 116
A Better Way: Sharing Leadership by Delegating 117
How to Delegate 120
Delegate Authority, Not Responsibility 122
Covering up or Fixing Problems Frustrates Delegation 122
Following Through 124
The Big Boss – the Opposite of Shared Leadership 126
Coaching and Mentoring 129
Shifting Gears – Situational Leadership 130
Being a Good Follower 131
Sharing Leadership through Consensus 135
Sharing Leadership by "Joining In" 136
Evaluating Leadership 136
Candid Self-Evaluation and Self-Assessment 137

Section 9
Techniques That Support the Patrol Method 139

Leading by Example: "Show Me" Leadership 141
Advancement: A Leadership Must 143
Building Trust 145
Beware of Parental Conflicts of Interest 146
Giving Direction 147
Good Communication 149
Storytelling: A Powerful Way to Communicate 152
Logical and Consistent Decisionmaking 154
Setting Priorities 156
Logic and Consistency 157

Representing the Team 158
Getting Input from the Team 161
Effective Teaching. 162
Own Your Leadership. 164
Discipline: Encouraging Others to Do Their Best 165
Praise and Recognition. 168
Celebrate Victories 171

Section 10
Create Your Personal Legacy of Leadership 173

Epilogue
Baden-Powell's Last Letter to Scouts 177

Appendix
To Learn More. 179

Troop Leadership Training (TLT). 181
Basic Troop Leadership Training Agenda. 181
Detailed Troop Leadership Training Weekend Model:. 182
Scout Oath 189
Scout Law 189
Scout Motto 189
Scout Slogan 189
Aims of Scouting. 191
The Methods of Scouting 191
William "Green Bar Bill" Hillcourt's
   "Ten Essentials of Scoutmastership" Reinterpreted 193
Difficulties in Working the Patrol Method. 195

Acknowledgements 197

Photograph and Illustration Credits 203

Foreword

The first morning at summer camp was rainy and new Scout Brian Smith had not slept well. His sleeping bag had slid halfway down his cot so the bottom half was outside the tent, soaking up the rain. One sock, a flashlight, two boots, a Scout neckerchief and a few other possessions lay on the wet ground behind the tent. Brian's Patrol Leader (who was also his tent mate) tried to get Brian to clean up, but Brian seemed to have no idea where to begin.

Brian's advancement schedule was just as disorganized as his tent. He had lost the blue merit badge cards Scoutmaster Kramer had signed, and the Archery and Leatherworking Merit Badge counselors were complaining. The Archery counselor, concerned about range safety, asked Scoutmaster Kramer whether Brian suffered from ADHD. Brian's Patrol Leader offered to accompany Brian to his classes and hand deliver a new set of cards directly to the counselors.

Despite his organizational challenges, by the end of the week Brian had completed all of his Tenderfoot requirements and now sat in uniform before his Board of Review. The Board members asked a few substantive questions and were pleasantly surprised at Brian's depth of knowledge.

"You've done well so far, Brian. What do you hope to accomplish in Scouting?" asked a Board member.

"I want to be an Eagle Scout," Brian replied.

"Why do you want to be an Eagle Scout?"

"Because I want to make a difference," said Brian, looking up at the canopy of leaves above him and fidgeting in his seat.

A pause. "Why will being an Eagle Scout help you make a difference?" asked another Board member, expecting an answer like "It will help me to get into college" or "because then I'll be able to boss the other kids around."

"Because Eagle Scouts make a difference," answered Brian. "If I become an Eagle Scout, I will be able to make more of a difference."

The Board members looked at one another in astonishment. From the mouth of this disorganized 11-year-old had come one of the most insightful comments they had ever heard from any Scout at any Board of Review.

We wrote this book to explore how Scout leaders can use Baden-Powell's Patrol Method to train Scouts to lead. We do not have all the answers. But we wanted to share practical lessons we have learned in our Scouting experiences in hopes that they may prove useful to other Scoutmasters, Assistant Scoutmasters, Venture Advisors and other adult leaders.

The Boy Scouts of America is America's most successful youth program. Our shared vision as Scout Leaders is to:

> *Offer young people responsible fun and adventure; Instill in young people lifetime values and develop in them ethical character as expressed in the Scout Oath and Law; Train young people in citizenship, service, and leadership; Serve America's communities and families with its quality, values-based program.*

> — BSA Vision Statement

The BSA carefully chose the language "Train young people in citizenship, service, and leadership." Not teach. Not encourage. Train.

Training and mentoring our Scouts in leadership may seem less important than "fun and adventure," "lifetime values," "ethical character," "citizenship" and "service." In the "business" of running an active Scout Troop, it is easy to let leadership training play second fiddle or even slip through the cracks. A Scoutmaster has strong incentives to favor orderliness and efficiency over leadership training. However, leadership training is part of our shared mission and has been central to Scouting since Baden-Powell created Scouting more than a century ago. It is more important now than ever.

Leadership training: aren't we doing that all the time? Not necessarily. Even if we are doing everything else right, training our Scouts to lead does not automatically follow. We need to do more than set a good example and be a good role model.

Leadership training and mentoring in a Scout troop is actually very simple. Any Scoutmaster who puts his mind to it can do it. Trust and respect your Scouts. Use the Patrol Method. Give your Scouts real responsibility. Mentor. Motivate. Recognize results.

While the basics are simple, the devil is in the details. In addition to understanding what to do, we also need practical tools and techniques to get the job done. A self-evaluation of our own leadership training efforts brought us back to the roots of Scouting: B-P's own life and writings. In B-P we found a practical man who had great insights that are still mostly valid today, a century after he first formulated them. We are convinced that B-P's ideas for the first Boy Scout Camp at Brownsea Island in the summer of 1907 are difficult to improve upon.

Our modest goal in writing this guide was to help bring ourselves and our fellow Scouters back to practicing Lord Baden-Powell's basic "game with a purpose" for leadership training. We offer the guideposts that have been most useful to us over the years: practical guidance from Baden-Powell himself. Just as B-P did, we illustrate practical techniques through storytelling—"Leadership Yarns."

We wrote this book for modern American Scout leaders. You can buy B-P's *Scouting for Boys* at your local BSA Scout Shop. Reprints of B-P's *Aids to Scoutmastership* are available at Amazon.com. B-P's books are wonderful and definitive, but can be tough going for modern American readers. In addition, while human beings have not changed much since B-P's time, certain practical techniques that worked for British boys of the early 1900's may need some re-positioning for modern American teenagers.

This guide is just a starting point. You probably have leadership experience from other contexts, although you may find that not everything you do at work or in the armed forces will directly translate into leading a Scout Troop. Talk to experienced Scoutmasters in your district. Go to your district's Scoutmaster training courses. Please attend your council's Wood Badge training course and earn your beads.

There is no substitute for experience. We think of Scouting as a laboratory for leadership training. A unit's weekend campouts and hikes, the important week or two at summer camp, the Patrol Leaders Council's Court of Honor planning session — everything a unit does, in fact — is a perfect opportunity for leadership training. In the outdoor laboratory that is Scouting, it's just you, at least one other uniformed leader or other adult, and your Scouts.

This book might get you thinking more about your own leadership training efforts. Reading it may give you some new ideas or a new perspective. It may help you to confirm what you already know works. Some of your practical solutions may be better than ours. Beyond B-P's basic Patrol Method precepts, there is no one right way of Scout leadership training. The important thing is to think about what we are doing and why we are doing it. Through focus and experience, you will soon develop instincts. Trust them.

If you have comments, insights, criticisms, or an experience to share, please drop us a line. We would love to hear from you. We know we will benefit from what you have to say.

Good luck in your Scouting adventures. You are a major participant in the greatest, most exciting, most effective youth program and movement ever created. We are a worldwide brotherhood whose defining characteristic is the Patrol Method — a mechanism Baden-Powell adopted to train youth to become effective, ethical, unselfish, dedicated leaders. This is exactly what America needs today. You can make it happen if you set your mind to it.

Introduction

We Are Often Distracted from Effective Scout Leadership Training and Mentoring

Any good Scoutmaster can tell you that running a Scout Troop is hard work. Volunteers are constantly "forgetting" to do the things they say they are going to do — or doing them only at the last minute when there is little margin for error. Logistics of organizing Troop events can be challenging. Scouts do not get together every day and may attend different schools, making communication and coordination difficult.

With 21st century achievement-oriented parents and their children demanding increasingly well organized and well-run, action-packed, entertaining programs, many Scoutmasters, Assistant Scoutmasters and Crew Advisors have chosen to rely heavily on capable adults to get things done efficiently, timely and correctly. After all, Scouts usually do not have the planning, organization and logistical skills to carry out complex Troop activities. If you want to have something done right, delegate it to someone who has done it before and has all the requisite skills. That's good leadership, right?

Consider our mission: to train Scouts to lead. If our Troop Committee and adult leaders do most of the planning and decision-making, the Scouts will have little responsibility. But Scouts can't learn how to lead just by following or watching. Learning to be a leader requires practice. In Scouting, achieving perfection is not nearly so important as letting the Scouts do it themselves.

It Takes Discipline and Focus to Be Effective

While nearly all Scoutmasters say they want to develop leadership qualities in their Scouts, far fewer seem to have spent much time thinking through how to actually do it. Even fewer are disciplined and focused enough to do an effective job of training Scouts to lead other Scouts.

Many believe leadership training automatically flows from other Scouting methods such as good advancement, or by having Scouts in uniform be "up front" conducting opening and closing ceremonies, or by sending one or two Scouts to council-run leadership training courses. Those things are necessary, but they are not enough.

A Scout Troop Is the Perfect Place to Mold and Mentor Leaders

The BSA is dedicated to training Scouts to be leaders. It offers Council-level, regional and National Scout leadership training programs. These programs are excellent. They can transform Scouts who go through them.

A Scoutmaster should encourage his Scouts to attend BSA leadership training courses. But he needs to do more. We unit leaders should not just sit back and let specialists at other levels of the Scouting organization take care of what is perhaps the most critical part of the mission. B-P intended *you* to train your Scouts to lead.

Leadership training is for all Scouts — not just the few who will attend council-level training programs. Baden-Powell believed leadership training should pervade the entire Scouting program. He created Patrols to offer leadership opportunities to as many Scouts as possible. That can happen only in a natural Scout Troop such as yours.

Nearly everything a Scout Troop does is an opportunity to train Scouts to lead. We Scoutmasters and Assistant Scoutmasters have a lot of time with our Scouts — at least a weekend each month, a night each week and a week at camp each summer. We know our Scouts better than any District or Council level leader ever will. The BSA has given us a mission: train Scouts to lead. We need to exercise careful focus, dedication and discipline if our unit's program is going to effectively train young leaders.

Leadership Training and Mentoring Is Hands-On, Not Theoretical

The only real way to learn how to lead is by doing it. Will Rogers once quipped,

"There are three kinds of men: The ones that learn by reading; The few who learn by observation; The rest of us have to pee on the electric fence and find out for ourselves."

People are more complex than electric fences. Figuring out how to motivate people and get them to follow you is the quest of a lifetime. How does a teenager get the opportunity to learn how to do that? By joining a Scout Troop! Scouting provides many opportunities for Scouts to learn how to lead by finding out for themselves — but only if Scoutmasters and other adult leaders make it happen.

Will Rogers was also saying that you probably will not learn how to train Scouts to lead simply by reading this or any other book. We have tried to keep this book very practical, but there is no substitute for experience. Your next Troop campout is the perfect opportunity to try out a new approach. Be patient with yourself. Keep trying. If you have the vision, focus and dedication, you cannot fail.

The Patrol Method Is the Recipe for Scout Leadership Training

Baden-Powell's Patrol Method is the recipe for youth leadership training. Weekend camping trips and weeklong treks or summer camps are concentrated leadership opportunities. There are many logistical, planning and other interesting leadership challenges to putting together a fun, active outdoor program. The younger boys instantly recognize the authority of the older boys because of the difference in ages and experience. Outdoor activities tend to provide immediate and direct feedback about what works and what does not.

Many Scouts Will Not Lead Without Encouragement from Their Scoutmasters

Many 21st century teenagers are perfectly willing to sit back and let adults take care of all the headaches. After all, in America's increasingly suburbanized lives, that is what most parents do with their teenagers — take care of all their problems and make all their decisions for them.

In a Scout Troop, the Scoutmaster sets the standard for leadership. Effective youth leadership training begins with the Scoutmaster.

We use the term leadership *training* throughout this book to differentiate it from "teaching" leadership or "instilling" leadership or "encouraging" Scouts to lead. Leadership training is not about using a whiteboard to conduct management classes. Training a Scout to lead is much more active. It requires lots of individualized attention, mentoring, guiding, pushing and prodding. Even more importantly, it takes judgment and experience to know when and how to intervene in a way that will not undercut leadership.

Leadership training is also a gradual process that takes time and patience. One can think of it as tending a garden. The gardener can prepare the ground, plant the seeds, weed regularly and even guide the way the plant stems are headed. But ultimately, it is up to the plants themselves to grow strong and tall.

Sometimes, too much or the wrong kind of intervention can actually hurt the growing plants.

Are You Prepared to Train and Mentor Tomorrow's Leaders?

Here are some interesting questions we ask ourselves from time to time:

* Do we believe ethical, effective leadership is important to America and the world?

* Are we committed to helping our Scouts become effective leaders?

* Are we willing to give our Scouts the opportunity to lead?

* Are we prepared to focus on applying the Patrol Method?

* Can we trust teenagers to lead "our" unit?

* Can we allow teenagers to learn from their own mistakes without trying to solve all their problems?

* Are we prepared to be the patient mentor and counselor — sitting in the back of the room rather than standing up in front?

* Do we have the time, commitment and dedication to give our Scouts the training and tools they need to lead effectively?

The Best Scoutmasters Are Stage Directors

Baden-Powell taught us that the best Scoutmasters are the ones who can retire to a corner of the meeting room or campsite and watch the activities move forward under the leadership of the Scouts themselves. This does not mean that the Scoutmaster's role is unimportant or minimized. Far from it! To the contrary, putting the Scouts out in front to make decisions and lead other Scouts is the highest credit to any Scoutmaster.

The best Scoutmasters we have seen spend most of their time behind the scenes — mentoring and guiding young leaders, educating parents and running interference to prevent other adults from taking responsibility away from Scouts. They train their Scouts to lead and then trust them with the responsibility of self-governance. Of course, any Scoutmaster occasionally needs to take charge and exercise authority — after all, boys will be boys. But the best Scoutmasters are careful about how and why they intervene. In this book you may find some pointers so you don't have to learn all your lessons the hard way.

How This Guide Is Organized

Section 1 "Understanding and Telling 'The Why' " describes a basic approach of logic and explanation in leadership and leadership training. American boys are more willing to be led when they understand the reason why they are being asked or told to do something.

Section 2 " 'The Why' of Scout Leadership Training" provides historical perspective on how B-P designed Scouting to train leaders. If you are new to Scouting, you may learn a lot from Section 2. If you already know all about Brownsea Island, you can skip to Section 3.

Sections 3 and 4 on "The Patrol Method" are the heart of this guide. These sections provide practical advice and guidance on how to use B-P's basic Patrol organizational structure and method to train Scouts how to lead other Scouts. If you read nothing else in this guide, you may want to spend some time with these sections.

Section 5 "Striving for Excellence: Doing Your Best" provides some inspirational explanation about the importance of doing our best along with techniques for motivating Scouts to do their best.

Section 6 "Caring Leadership" discusses the role of ethical decision-making in training Scouts to become leaders. Ethical servant leadership is the starting point for the "Be-Know-Do" principles underlying modern Scout leadership training. Unethical or immoral leadership is far worse than no leadership at all. We can show our Scouts through our example what it means to act ethically. We can make ethical considerations a part of every important decision.

Section 7 "Planning: How to Facilitate Without Taking Over" provides practical guidance on how to get inexperienced planners to plan more effectively and accomplish goals. Planning is a life skill. It is also an essential part of modern Scout leadership training. Effective leadership cannot take place without it. Planning is usually where Scoutmasters have the most difficulty when they are trying to create a Scout-run Troop. The typical fifteen-year old has no idea how to plan, and yet is expected in a Scout-run Troop to plan for many other people including adults.

Section 8 "Shared Leadership" explores delegating, situational leadership and other ways to share leadership.

Section 9 "Techniques that Support the Patrol Method" is a series of special topics we have found useful in training leaders.

Section 10 "Create Your Personal Legacy of Leadership" steps back and gives a long-term perspective.

The Appendix includes information that may be useful to you, including some ideas for Troop Leadership Training weekend experiences.

Look for "leadership compass bearings" to help you orient yourself on your journey.

Each section contains quotations from Baden-Powell's original source materials as well as additional quotations we have found helpful or inspirational.

You will also find storytelling "Leadership Yarns." Baden-Powell knew that storytelling is one of the most effective ways to communicate ideas. Our "Leadership Yarn" stories are fictional but are loosely based on composite observations we have made along the way or heard from other Scout leaders. Any resemblance of the fictional characters in our "Leadership Yarns" to real people is purely coincidental.

In our experience, the best way to train Scouts how to lead is out in the field, not in a classroom. Scouts get more than enough classroom time in school. We cannot imagine B-P telling a group of Scouts to sit down in front of a chalkboard or even a television set for a presentation on effective personnel management. He used campouts, hikes, patrol meetings and campfires as practical opportunities to train Scouts how to lead. In our experience, it is highly effective to teach Scouts leadership on a practical as-needed basis when they need a particular technique or realization to solve a problem. If we are doing our Scoutmaster job correctly, our Scouts will constantly present us with "teaching moments" we can use to advance leadership training.

If you have completed Wood Badge for the 21st Century, you may notice that this guide is sparse on the memory tips of the BSA's current Youth Leadership

Training Continuum. This guide is closely aligned with the spirit of National Youth Leadership Training and complements NYLT's detailed methods, skills, tools and philosophy. However, we are starting from a somewhat more traditional perspective: our founder, B-P's, own writings. For in-depth discussion of modern BSA leadership theory and practice, we encourage you to read your BSA Scoutmaster's Handbook and other excellent course and leadership training materials the BSA offers — or even better, enroll in your council's next Wood Badge for the 21st Century course. Just remember B-P's admonition: if you follow the Patrol Method and do your best, you cannot fail!

For more information and other resources, point your web browser to our website www.Scoutleadership.com. It offers helpful links, additional materials and other resources.

Most of all, have fun! You are an important part of the most successful youth organization the world has ever known. We are all fortunate to be Scout Leaders in 21st century America.

People are more willing to be led when they understand the reason why they are being asked to do something. As a leader, be sure to explain why you want someone to do something. You may be surprised at the results.

Understanding and Telling "The Why"

Leadership Yarn ⚬⚬⚬⚬⚬⚬⚬⚬⚬⚬⚬⚬⚬⚬⚬⚬⚬⚬⚬⚬⚬⚬⚬⚬⚬⚬⚬⚬⚬⚬⚬⚬

Troop 49's newly-elected Senior Patrol Leader Jared Sayer knew exactly what he liked and what he did not like. Jared liked himself quite a lot. What he did not like was incompetence, laziness and excuses. He was tired of Patrol Leaders who do not do what they say they are going to do, Scouts who do not work hard to learn new skills, and adults who stand in the way of progress. Jared was disappointed with mostly everyone in Troop 49. "A lot is going to change now that I'm SPL," Jared promised himself.

Jared ran his first few Troop meetings and his first Patrol Leaders Council meeting with authority. He stood up in front of the room and did all the talking. He expected his subordinates to listen carefully to each pearl of wisdom he thoughtfully bestowed. Jared wasn't interested in what his Patrol Leaders, or anyone else (including his Scoutmaster Robert Johnson) had to say. Jared had it all figured out.

Soon after becoming Senior Patrol Leader, Jared asked to sit for his Life Board of Review. Scoutmaster Johnson gave Committee Chair Gonzales, who would chair the Life Board, a "heads up" that the Board might want to focus some of its inquiry on leadership. Mr. Gonzales, in turn, talked beforehand with Jared's parents, who agreed to fully support any decision the Board might reach. After Jared had correctly recited the Scout Oath and Law, Mr. Gonzales dug right in. He asked Jared to define the Patrol Method.

"The Patrol Method is the chain of command," Jared said confidently.

"What do you mean by 'chain of command?'" Mr. Gonzales asked.

"The Senior Patrol Leader issues the orders, and everyone else follows them," Jared replied with authority. "That's what we mean by Scout-run."

"What if a Patrol Leader disagrees with the Senior Patrol Leader's orders?" Mr. Gonzales inquired.

"Too bad," said Jared. "The Senior Patrol Leader was elected to his position and is in charge of the Troop. What he says goes. He's the leader. You must always follow the leader."

"What about the Patrol Leaders Council?" asked Ms. Sims, who had remained active with the Troop Committee long after her son made Eagle. "Can the Patrol Leaders overrule the Senior Patrol Leader?"

"Ma'am, the Patrol Leaders Council is supposed to follow the Senior Patrol Leader," Jared responded, a little impatiently. "PLC meetings are how the Senior Patrol Leader gives orders to his Patrol Leaders. A Patrol Leader who refuses to follow his Senior Patrol Leader should be removed from his position."

"Have you ever asked the Patrol Leaders Council to vote?" asked Mr. Gonzales.

"No," Jared responded confidently. "I never needed to. My Patrol Leaders have never once disagreed with anything I decided the Troop would do."

Jared was shocked when the Board announced its decision: Jared was not yet ready for Life Scout.

"You're joking! Why not?" Jared cried indignantly, his face flushed and his pride wounded.

"Mr. Sayers, you have some things to learn about leadership," Mr. Gonzales responded. "I'm not sure where to begin. I suggest you spend some time with Scoutmaster Johnson. We'll expect to see you in about three months."

Jared swallowed his pride and began talking with Scoutmaster Johnson about leadership. Jared learned many lessons over the next three months. It was a rocky trail, but Scoutmaster Johnson mentored him every step along the way. Jared got to know his Patrol Leaders and realized they weren't so bad after all. They tried hard, even though they did not always succeed. Jared matured and became less self-centered. He began to realize that being Senior Patrol Leader was not all about him after all.

After three months, Scoutmaster Johnson asked Jared if he felt ready to sit for a continuation of his Life Board. "I think you are nearly ready, Jared" announced Mr. Johnson. "But first, I want you to talk to Sergeant Brown about 'The Why.'" Mr. Johnson took Jared over to meet First Sergeant Brown, an Eagle alumnus of Troop 49 who was home from active duty for the holidays.

"Maurice, I think you know our Senior Patrol Leader Jared Sayers." Jared shook hands with Sergeant Brown. "Jared has an important Board of Review coming up," Mr. Johnson explained. "Can you spend a few minutes explaining your take on the fundamentals of leadership?"

Sergeant Brown explained to Jared how a leader accomplishes his objective by working through other people, and that the team working together is far stronger *than any team member working by himself. He explained why it is important to lead from the front, and why a leader needs to set the example. Brown explained that the goal of leadership is to make the team strong and effective, and that a leader does not get there by acting out of self-importance or by trying to control everyone. Brown emphasized how a leader has to earn the loyalty and respect of his followers. He explained how loyalty flows both up and down and is a two-way street. He explained why a leader must be loyal to each member of his team.*

Sergeant Brown talked about respect. He explained why a leader must know the strengths and weaknesses of each member of his team, and what makes each of them tick. He talked about why a leader must have humility, and why he must connect with every member of his team. Brown explained that out there in the world, "stuff happens" and that a leader must adjust his style to the situation.

Brown continued for twenty-five minutes. Jared listened intently. Some of the things Brown was saying were new to Jared, but he immediately understood their importance now that he had a hard few months of leadership experience under his belt. For him, it was as if pieces of a jigsaw puzzle were falling into place. Jared finally "got it." Perhaps not all of it, but enough to match up with his experiences. Jared was now ready for his Life Board. He understood "The Why."

When Jared sat for his Board, everyone noticed how Jared had changed. When Mr. Gonzales asked him about the Patrol Method, Jared volunteered, "Sir, I had it all wrong last time." Jared went on to describe what he had learned and practiced. Jared readily admitted that he still had a lot more to learn. His demeanor was humble and relaxed. "Jared the Big Boss" was no more. It was no longer all about him. He was now a more effective leader. Jared passed his Life Board with flying colors, and went on to become an Eagle Scout.

> *"Lead, follow or get out of the way."*
>
> — Thomas Paine, American Patriot

> *"Don't Tread On Me"*
>
> — Gadsden Patriot Flag, American Revolutionary War

Some say developing a vision is the difference between managing and leading. But an American leader needs more than vision. He needs to communicate his vision to his followers in ways they can understand and adopt as their own.

"The genius of this [American] nation is not in the least to be compared with that of the Prussians, Austrians or French. You [in Europe] say to your soldier, 'Do this,' and he does it. [Here in America] I am obliged to say 'This is the reason why you ought to do that,' and then he does it."

— Baron Friedrich Wilhelm Augustus von Steuben,
Drillmaster of the Continental Army serving under
General George Washington at Valley Forge, 1778

We as an American people value our freedom above all else. We generally do not like to be told what to think or what to do. In a volunteer organization centered around preparing modern American teenagers to make ethical and moral choices over their lifetimes, effective leadership and leadership training needs to take these important factors into account.

Leadership Is Based on Trust

Modern American teenagers generally do not follow commands without question. World experiences of the 20th century have taught modern Americans to "question authority". We are more willing to trust those who lead us through logic, clarity, focus and understanding. We become uncomfortable when a leader's decisions seem to be based on emotion without rational thinking. We become nervous when a leader keeps us in the dark by not explaining the logic behind a decision or policy. We become suspicious when we detect hidden agendas that may not necessarily benefit the group as a whole. These considerations go to the heart of what it means to be an effective leader and an effective follower.

Telling "The Why" Helps Build Trust

Once vision and policy are set, how much information do leaders need to communicate to their followers about their common objective? The right answer is probably "it depends".

We can all think of situations where, for good reasons that clearly benefit the group as a whole, a leader may choose not to communicate certain information. However, depending on how important the issue is, trust usually goes only so far. We have a right to expect our leaders to be clear about why they are leading us in a particular direction. We may not always agree with a leader's "why".

However, even when we do not agree, most of us will follow our leader if we are convinced he is leading in a manner that is logical, rational and based on a policy he can explain is for the common good.

The more information we have about "The Why", the more effective and helpful we can be in our role as followers. If we have no idea why a leader is asking us to do something, we may follow orders but we probably will not be very enthusiastic or effective. If a leader is unable or unwilling to tell us "The Why", we may even become suspicious. In a democratic society or a volunteer organization, we may refuse to follow until the leader tells us "The Why". Even in situations where orders are expected to be followed, persuasively and effectively telling "The Why" may be the single most important thing a leader can do to make his plan successful.

Clear Rational Thinking and Communication

Scoutmasters need to be very clear about what they are doing and why they are doing it. There can be no vision without clear thinking. We need to communicate our clarity to our Scout and adult leaders in a way that is effective and persuasive. To do this, it helps to know a lot about "The Why" of Scouting. A Scoutmaster needs to have the vision and clarity to "deliver the promise." You might want to re-read "The Promise of Scouting" in the Scout Handbook. Our mission as Scoutmasters is to deliver that Promise of Scouting to our Scouts. We also should apply the Aims and Methods of Scouting. (See Appendix and your Scoutmaster's Handbook.)

It is easy to be distracted by the many details and responsibilities that come with the Scoutmaster's shoulder patch. Focus. Think about the mission. Talk with others. Get trained. Make sure leadership training is always a big part of your program.

How much should a Scoutmaster tell his Scouts about "The Why" of Scouting? Some Scoutmasters think Scouts will be less interested once they realize "the game" actually has a purpose. Many Scoutmasters wonder how much children can really understand about long-term strategies such as building good character and learning how to lead effectively.

Self-discovery can be a powerful and effective way to learn. People like their own ideas. Someone who comes to a realization or learns a lesson on his own (even if he is led to it) is more likely to take that lesson to heart and use it in the future.

But people generally do not like to be asked to do something for no reason or "just because." This is especially true in voluntary organizations in America, where leadership based solely on power or control is rarely effective. Most people generally trust their leaders, but also feel they have a right to be told what is going on and why.

Tell "The Why"

People are more willing to be led when they understand the reason why they are being asked to do something. As a leader, be sure to explain why you want someone to do something. You may be surprised at the results.

Some Scoutmasters seem to assume their Scouts do not care what is really going on or do not need to know. Lengthy discussions with 16 and 17-year-old Senior Scouts around many campfires have taught us how deeply Scouts care about Troop elections, Troop decision making, whether they are being given real authority, and other important issues relating to Troop leadership and organization. Any Scoutmaster who misjudges the sophistication of 21st century teenagers is in for a big surprise.

In the shared leadership environment of a Scout Troop, Scouts who understand "The Why" are likely to participate more enthusiastically than those who feel they are simply being "bossed around" or being subjected to the arbitrary whims of someone who has power over them. If a leader cannot articulate a clear "why" for a task or effort, then he needs to reconsider why he is making the request. In a Scout Troop, virtually all tasks involving youth should have "leadership training" as one of the "whys."

Leadership Yarn

Two Scouts were overheard talking about their former Senior Patrol Leader.

"Remember the time," said one, "Dan told us all to set up camp at the bottom of the hill and then a few minutes later he made us move camp to the top of the hill?"

"Yeah," said the other, "I never understood why he did that. It was like he got a kick out of ordering us around."

"Maybe he realized our campsite would get washed away in a rainstorm if we stayed in the original place," said the first Scout.

"Well, if that had been the reason, he should have told us. I never understood why that guy did anything he did," said the other Scout. He looked around, and then said in a lower voice, "I'm so glad he's not our Senior Patrol Leader anymore. Kevin sometimes makes mistakes, but at least he tells us why he wants us to do stuff."

Teaching Moments

As Scoutmasters, one of our duties is to meet with every Scout as he seeks promotion to a higher rank. The "Scoutmaster's Conference" is an excellent time to discuss "The Why" of Scouting with our Scouts.

Leadership Yarn

Jimmy, a new Scout, recently bridged over from Webelos and was eager to demonstrate his knowledge. He wanted to earn the rank of Scout. He had memorized everything he was supposed to — the Scout Oath and Law, how to tie a square knot, the meaning of the Scout Badge, and all the other requirements. He dressed neatly in his new uniform, brought his Handbook to the meeting and sat with his Scoutmaster. He was very good. He could recite it all. His square knot was tight and square.

"Well Jimmy, are you excited about joining the Troop?" asked Scoutmaster Wong.

"Yes, sir!" Jimmy said enthusiastically.

"You learned all of the requirements for the rank of Scout. You worked very hard. I am pleased to welcome you to our Troop. Good job! But tell me — why do you want to become a Boy Scout?"

Jimmy knew all the requirements cold, but he had never thought about "why" he wanted to become a Scout. "Well, I was a Cub Scout. Being a Boy Scout is fun and I like camping," he blurted out.

"That's wonderful! We do have a lot of fun. We love to camp. In fact, our Troop goes camping every month. Those are great reasons to be a Scout!" said the Scoutmaster.

Scoutmaster Wong paused a moment. He thought about whether this particular Scout was ready to go on to the next level, and decided to proceed. He knew Jimmy's father was an Eagle Scout, and that he and Jimmy's mother were great supporters of the Scouting program. "How about the Scout Oath and Law you just took? What do they mean to you, Jimmy?" Scoutmaster Wong asked.

Jimmy definitely was not ready for this question. However, Scoutmaster Wong decided this was a good chance to lay the foundation to discuss important issues with Jimmy in later Scoutmaster Conferences. Scoutmaster Wong would continue to learn what Jimmy thought about various issues of Scouting that are not in the requirements, but are important nonetheless.

By asking these questions, Scoutmaster Wong also hoped to begin establishing a relationship of mutual trust and respect that would eventually transcend the shared experience of having fun on camping trips. The Scoutmaster knew such respectful relationships could make a big difference later on should a Scout ever find himself in trouble or in need of advice.

Leadership Yarn 〰〰〰〰〰〰〰〰〰〰〰〰〰〰〰〰〰〰〰〰〰〰

When Bill's son joined the Troop, Bill also joined and began serving on Troop and National Boards of Review for advancing Scouts.

During his work on Boards of Review, Bill developed a thoughtful line of examination that required each candidate to consider the meaning of his board and why he wanted to advance and the role he saw Scouting playing in his life. He got the candidate to consider the many "whys" of his Scouting experience. Bill was an inspiration to the Scouts as well as to the other adults who served on the boards with him.

Telling "The Why" Is Important

Without understanding "The Why," leadership in a voluntary, shared leadership environment such as Scouting will often fail. Some may challenge this assertion with examples where a more authoritative approach is called for. In military actions and emergencies, it is often important to follow orders without questioning them or understanding "The Why." "The Why" is usually already understood.

Think of the combat soldier ordered to go out on patrol. He does not need an explanation of "why" — he knows why he is there and what his mission is. Think of the first responders at a car wreck who direct someone to dial 9-1-1 and summon help for the injured. The first responders who ran into the World Trade Center towers after the 2001 attack on our nation *knew "The Why."*

B-P talked about "a game with a purpose." The purpose is "The Why." As leaders, we understand "The Why" as our shared mission to train future citizens and leaders of our nation. This is "The Why" at a strategic, organizational level. However, we also need to clearly explain what we are doing and why, to those whom we expect to implement our designs.

Most times in Scouting, leaders should rely on logic. If a primary purpose of Scouting is to share leadership and train new leaders, then articulating "The Why" is an excellent way for older Scouts to train younger Scouts to be leaders. Under this shared leadership approach, the leader articulates *why* he wants others to perform certain tasks. It has to make sense to his followers.

Leadership Yarn

Star Scout Dylan Keenan was the most senior Scout attending the Troop's Brownsea Camp for new Scouts. Dylan had relatively little leadership experience, but he was strong on values. He was raised in a very religious household, and he took the Scout Oath and Law literally and tried to live his life by them.

First Class Scout Jordan Smith was your average kid from a broken home. Jordan's father worked construction and had lived a tough life. Jordan's father swore incessantly, so it was no wonder that Jordan had also picked up the habit of sprinkling his conversations with a colorful word or two.

Keenan and Smith were putting up a tarp for a fire-building demonstration. As they jockeyed the poles and lines, one of the stakes suddenly pulled out and the tarp collapsed. Without thinking, Smith mumbled an expletive under his breath, and then set about trying to drive the stake back into the ground so it would hold.

Keenan was incensed at Smith's blatant violation of the 11th point of the Scout Law. "Hey, watch your mouth!" said Keenan sharply. "You're a Scout! Apologize!"

Smith was surprised by Keenan's reaction. "Come on, Dylan, nobody heard me. Relax," said Smith. However, Keenan would not let it drop — to him it was a matter of principle.

"I heard you. That was enough. I'm a Star Scout. And I'm acting Senior Patrol Leader on this camping trip. You have to do as I say. And I say you need to apologize."

Keenan's attempt to pull rank got Smith mad. As blood rushed to his face, Jordan Smith looked Dylan Keenan in the eye with fury and said "Look Keenan, just because you have one more merit badge than me doesn't give you the right to boss

me around. If you want this $&%^$ tarp up, you can $%%* put it up yourself!"
Smith threw down the tent stake and stalked away.*

*Keenan followed him across the campsite. "Didn't you hear what I said?" yelled
Keenan. "Apologize!" Smith just kept on walking.*

*Keenan went right to Scoutmaster Bergen. He complained about Smith's behavior
and insubordination. But the Scoutmaster had watched the entire exchange from
a distance. And his reaction was not at all what Keenan expected.*

*"Dylan, I admire your integrity and dedication to Scout Values," said Scoutmaster
Bergen. "Jordan shouldn't use that kind of language. No Scout should. But let me
ask you this. Do you think your interaction with Jordan was effective?"*

*Effective? Keenan admitted that he had accomplished nothing. "How could you
have done it differently?" asked Mr. Bergen. "I have no idea," said Keenan.*

*"Have you ever thought of talking about the swearing issue around the campfire
after the younger boys go to bed? Maybe have a heart to heart with Jordan about
swearing and its effect on the younger Scouts?"*

*Keenan said this had never occurred to him. "Dylan, sometimes boys swear be-
cause they want to sound more like adults," explained Scoutmaster Bergen. "It was
just you and Jordan over there — no younger Scouts were within earshot. Jordan
is not going to listen to you just because you say you're in charge. To work any
change, you're probably going to have to use your powers of persuasion. Ordering
him not to swear will get you nowhere. Besides, he has served as a Patrol Leader
and is a good leader in his own right. Trying to pull rank on him is not going to
work. I think you need to tell him 'The Why.' He may not agree, but you might get
him to think about it."*

We have talked about telling "The Why." The next Section provides historical
perspective on "The Why" of Scout leadership training. Our founder, Robert
Baden-Powell, always intended Scouting to be a way to train boys to lead. He
designed the very first Scout summer camp at Brownsea Island as an experiment in youth leadership training. Understanding this historical perspective
provides focus and vision to deliver B-P's promise of training boys to become
the future leaders of our nation.

Ernest Thompson Seton, Robert Baden-Powell, and Daniel C. Beard

"The Why" of Scout Leadership Training
(The True Yarn of Baden-Powell on Brownsea Island)

"That's what you learn in the Boy Scouts: Somebody's got to take command here; now whoever it's going to be, what are we going to do next? And he says what we're going to do next, and off you go. … they are the children of democracy. And if democracy is under attack, they'll go out and fight for it."

— Interview with the late Stephen Ambrose, historian and author

The Game with a Purpose

"Green Bar" Bill Hillcourt wrote in one of his essays on Scouting that:

"To a boy, Scouting is a game, a magnificent game, full of play and full of laughter, keeping him busy, keeping him happy. That is the strength of Scouting! A boy becomes a Scout for the sheer fun there is in it."

As Green Bar Bill well knew (and went on to explain in this same essay), Scouting is much more than this. Many youth organizations offer fun and adventure. Scouting is different. Why?

> **Baden-Powell said:**
>
> **"We are not a club — nor a Sunday school — but a school of the woods."**

Baden-Powell did not think much of the classroom. B-P's "school of the woods" was not a classroom under the tree canopy — it is what we now call the "outdoor program" of learning through outdoor experience. In addition to learning about outdoor skills and self-reliance, the most important thing a Scout can do in the outdoors is to figure out how to lead other Scouts. The outdoors has an immediacy and directness that makes it an excellent laboratory for youth leadership training.

To understand "The Why" of Scouting, it is important to know something about the truly extraordinary person who founded Scouting — R.S.S. Baden-Powell, Lord of Gilwell, or as all Scouts knew him, "B-P".

Baden-Powell was the right man at the right time. As a middle-aged retired British Army general officer and war hero, he took lessons he learned at boarding school and in the military and used them to formulate the single most successful youth program in history.

The Inception of Scouting's Outdoor Program

Robert Baden-Powell

While attending the Charterhouse boarding school outside of London as a boy in the mid-19th century, B-P spent as much time as he could out in a copse of woods on the school grounds. He loved to "hide out" in a wooded area down a hill and away from the pitches and halls of his beloved school. Sometimes he would catch rabbits and roast them over an open fire he built himself. Other times, he would climb trees and observe everything around him.

After graduating from Charterhouse, Baden-Powell joined the British Army. He spent most of his time in India and South Africa. As a young officer, Baden-Powell believed his troops always had to know what the enemy was doing. This required "Scouts" to follow the enemy and spy on them. B-P's idea of spying was not at all like what you might have seen in a James Bond movie. What he had in mind was traveling alone or in small groups in the backcountry (often under cover of darkness), camping out under the stars, being highly observant, and avoiding detection.

Baden-Powell's "army Scouts" had to know how to travel light and live off the land. However, B-P was surprised to find out how many of the men under his command did not know how to be self-reliant in the outdoors. They lacked basic outdoor skills such as how to camp out, how to build a fire and how to cook for themselves. They did not know how to travel in a way to elude the enemy, or how to track and observe. Most importantly, they had to learn how to work together as a "patrol" — the origin of the B-P's "Patrol Method" for Boy Scouts.

B-P spent years training his "army Scouts" in the field. He eventually wrote a book called *Aids to Scouting* to train men how to be "Scouts" in time of war. B-P published his book in England just as he was given a new, important responsibility — defending the town of Mafeking in what is now the Republic of South Africa during the Boer War.

Giving Boys Important Responsibilities and Uniforms

Baden-Powell was in charge of a regiment of British soldiers defending Mafeking during a siege. The Boers surrounded the town so supplies could not get in. The Boers attacked Mafeking by shelling it from a distance in the hope that the town would eventually be forced to surrender.

The Boers laid siege to B-P's small garrison defending the town. To withstand the siege, everyone had to work together. As Baden-Powell lost some of his men to enemy action, he turned to the boys of the town for help. Of course, B-P did not give boys frontline combat roles, but he did ask them to do some of the less dangerous things needed to keep the town running. B-P trusted boys to do tasks that men had done before.

Charterhouse c. 1872: Robert Baden-Powell (center).

One of B-P's officers formed the boys into a cadet corps, gave them uniforms to wear, and had them take over jobs such as delivering messages, running the post office and keeping a lookout. These early "Boy Scout" prototypes served their town wonderfully. B-P learned from them first-hand that boys could perform admirable service and were capable of doing all sorts of important work.

After nearly ten months, the Boers finally realized that Mafeking under Baden-Powell's leadership was never going to surrender. They gave up their siege. The garrison defending the town was relieved. Back home, all of England had been reading about the siege in the newspapers — and everyone was jubilant that B-P and his men withstood the siege for so long. When B-P returned home to England, much to his surprise, he was welcomed as a national war hero.

Meanwhile, *Aids to Scouting* was being read widely by Britain's youth — boys and girls alike. Baden-Powell knew his book was not suitable for young people. It was directed to soldiers, not boys and girls. He decided to rewrite the book so it would be appropriate for both youth and peacetime.

Baden-Powell said:

"A small book [Aids to Scouting] which I published a short time ago on the subject of Scouting for soldiers has been so freely taken up by schools and boys' clubs in England that I am encouraged to think a system organised for the special purpose of teaching boys would be acceptable, and I am still further encouraged in the idea by the fact that a somewhat similar organization founded by Mr. Ernest Thompson Seton in America has had a full and widespread success... The whole intention of the Boy Scouts' training is for peaceful citizenship."

Baden-Powell's Great Experiment on Brownsea Island

No one had proposed anything like Scouting before. Some people (including his publisher) were skeptical that Baden-Powell's plan would actually work. Some people did not believe boys could live up to the responsibility of leading themselves. B-P himself did not have much experience with youth — after all, he had spent his entire life in the British Army. B-P decided to test his theories in practice. He wanted to find out:

* Would boys accept high levels of responsibility?

* Could leadership be taught using the "Patrol System" in an outdoor setting?

* Under the Patrol Method, would boys from different class backgrounds and experiences work together for the common good?

* Could boys live "on their honor" by a code of values and conduct?

* Would the boys have fun and enjoy themselves in learning these lessons?

Beginning on July 29, 1907, Baden-Powell at age 50, his first Assistant Scoutmaster and longtime friend Kenneth MacLaren and two other Assistant Scoutmasters (George Greene and Henry Robson) took 20 boys in four patrols out camping for twelve days on an island called "Brownsea" off the Dorset coast in southern England. With his newfound recognition, B-P obtained permission from the wealthy owners to conduct the very first "Boy Scout" summer camp on their island. Brownsea Island is large (it takes 30 minutes to walk across it) and takes a boat to get to. As a boy, B-P had sailed with his brothers from Poole Harbor to the beaches of this private island. B-P selected a part of the island facing away from Poole to set up his camp. The area has a good beach, some flat areas for campsites, and many wooded and swampy areas for adventures.

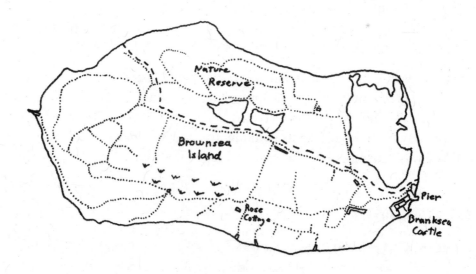

Map of Brownsea Island

B-P invited boys aged 10 to 17 (the average age was 14) from different walks of life to participate in his great experiment. Some of the boys were sons of B-P's friends in the military and had attended private high schools such as Eton and Charterhouse. Others were the sons of common laborers recruited from the "Boys Brigades" of the nearby towns of Bournemouth and Poole. Before coming to camp, B-P expected each boy to learn how to tie three specific knots (square knot, sheet bend and clove hitch). B-P also expected each boy to know how to swim.

When all Scouts had reported to camp, B-P divided the Scouts into four patrols. B-P chose names for the first Scout patrols ever: the Wolves, the Bulls, the Curlews and the Ravens. B-P seeded each patrol with boys of different backgrounds and experiences. B-P deliberately separated brothers into different patrols. He mixed town boys with "public school" boys in each patrol.

 B-P selected the four Patrol Leaders from among the public school Scouts in attendance. B-P issued the four Patrol Leaders special hats with white fleur-de-lis symbols. All the other Scouts received similar hats without Patrol Leader emblems.

B-P issued each patrol a triangular patrol flag mounted to a staff. B-P himself had painted green outlines of the appropriate bird or animal on the white cloth patrol flags. B-P also issued distinctively colored patrol shoulder knots to each boy. This way, each patrol had its own identity and anyone could tell which patrol a boy was a member of simply by looking at the color of his shoulder knot.

We do not know what criteria B-P used to choose his Patrol Leaders, but we can be sure that he made his decisions based on which boys he thought would make the best leaders. While the boys B-P chose were generally older, he did not always choose the oldest boy in each patrol to be Patrol Leader:

The 16-year-old Patrol Leader of the Wolves Patrol, Bob Wroughton, led four other Scouts aged 12-14 years old.

B-P selected 14-year-old Tom Evans-Lombe to lead the four other Scouts in the Bulls Patrol whose ages ranged from 10 to 15 years old.

15-year-old George Rodney led the Curlews Patrol consisting of four other Scouts aged 13 to 17.

16-year-old Herbert Emley was Patrol Leader of the Ravens comprising four other Scouts aged 10 through 16.

Unlike most modern Scout Troops, there was no "Senior Patrol Leader" or equivalent officer at Brownsea — the four Patrol Leaders were the leaders of the "Troop." The largest Brownsea patrol (the Wolves) consisted of only six Scouts, with the other patrols comprising five Scouts each. B-P did not have any concept that a patrol must comprise 8 to 10 Scouts, nor did he think a "Senior Patrol Leader" was necessary for the efficient operation of the Troop at Brownsea Island.

On the first day of camp, B-P conducted a special Patrol Leader's training session. We don't know everything B-P did or said during that first Scout leadership training, but we know that B-P told each Patrol Leader that he was to be fully responsible for his patrol at all times.

Baden-Powell said:

"Each Patrol Leader was given full responsibility for the behaviour of his patrol at all times, in camp and in the field. The patrol was the unit for work or play, and each patrol was camped in a separate spot."

The Brownsea Scout Patrols camped out in tents in separate areas, ate as patrols, played games as patrols, and learned new skills as patrols — all the activities we still do in Scout camp today. Each night at Brownsea, B-P assigned a different patrol to bivouac some distance away from the rest of the group and to serve as a night watch. This gave the bivouacking patrol a chance to operate entirely autonomously and prepare its own evening meal.

B-P planned each day's activities at Brownsea on an organizing theme. Each morning, B-P awakened the entire camp by blowing a kudu antelope horn he had brought back from Africa's Somabula Forest. The Scouts got up, washed themselves, drank some hot cocoa, cleaned up the campsite, and were called to assembly. B-P personally led the Scouts in an exercise drill and then presented the themes of the day — often through demonstrations. After a morning flag ceremony and prayers, the patrols sat down to eat breakfast under a central dining fly. Once breakfast and cleanup were over, the Scouts spent the morning working on new skills.

One day, the Scouts made huts and mattresses, tied knots, lit fires, baked bread, practiced sanitation skills, and learned about finding their way in unfamiliar terrain.

Another day, the topics were woodcraft, nature study, and noticing details of people to figure out their characters and actions.

Still another day was devoted to first aid and emergency preparedness. Another day focused on good citizenship, flag study and historical exercises.

There was a whole day devoted to tracking and observation. B-P dedicated another day to chivalry, honor, unselfishness, service to others, and doing a good turn daily.

B-P's 1907 Camp at Brownsea Island

The last day of camp was a field day — sports, games, competitions and the Scouts demonstrating what they had learned at camp.

B-P's Brownsea formula was to introduce a topic through stories ("yarns") and discussions at a campfire the night before. He then arranged for a demonstration the next morning before breakfast. The Scouts spent the rest of the morning working on their skills (learning by doing).

After lunch, the patrols competed against one another in competitions and games that required them to use the skills they learned during morning skill instruction. The Scouts did not know in advance what the competitions would be, so they needed to be resourceful and work together to compete successfully.

After dinner, B-P finished the Brownsea day with a campfire. At the campfire, the Brownsea Scouts sang songs, shouted cheers and listened to B-P's "yarns" about his experiences in India and South Africa. B-P would also use the campfire to introduce and discuss substantive topics for the next day's activities.

Baden-Powell said:

"We found the best way of imparting theoretical instruction was to give it out in short instalments with ample illustrative examples when sitting round the camp fire or otherwise resting, and with demonstrations in the practice hour before breakfast. A formal lecture is apt to bore the boys. The practice was then carried out in competitions and schemes."

As the Scouts at Brownsea became proficient in new skills, B-P awarded them brass fleur-de-lis badges to wear on their clothing. B-P chose the fleur-de-lis because it represented "North" on a mariner's compass and pointed the way. Initially all of the boys were "Tenderfeet." Once a boy demonstrated proficiency in certain skills, B-P awarded him the bottom half of a brass fleur-de-lis badge with the appellation of "Second Class Scout." If the boy demonstrated additional proficiency, he received the top half of the brass badge and was recognized as "First Class Scout." B-P made the original Scout badges himself.

The last afternoon at Brownsea, the island's owners invited the boys to tea at the castle. The boys then returned to camp for a closing campfire, where according to a journalist who was present, B-P answered questions, imitated birdcalls, showed the Scouts how to stalk an animal, told yarns, sang songs and led the Scouts in cheers.

Baden-Powell's experimental camp was a huge success. The Scouts loved it. The Patrol Leaders gladly accepted responsibility for the conduct of their patrols, and all the boys learned about outdoor skills and leadership. The Brownsea experience convinced B-P that he had found just the right recipe.

Baden-Powell said:

"Since this experimental camp I am more than ever convinced of the possibilities which underlie the Scouts' training as an educator for boys of all classes. Prepared as I was for the enthusiastic endeavour on the part of the lads, I was surprised at the effect on their character, which became visible even in the few days we were at work... That the boys enjoyed the training is evident from the letters which I have had from them..."

The following year, B-P wrote and began publishing what became the first Boy Scout Handbook. He called it *Scouting for Boys*. It was an instant best seller. First published in installments in a magazine, an estimated 25,000 boys and girls read it nearly overnight as soon as it came out and immediately wanted to become Scouts.

Scouting Caught on in the USA and All Over the World

The roots of Scouting in America grew from the seed of the British experience. We think every American Scout should know the story of publisher William Boyce, who became disoriented in London fog. Boyce grew up on a farm just outside of Pittsburgh, and became a successful Chicago newspaper magnate. He was also an avid outdoorsman and world traveler. He had built his successful weekly newspaper empire by using a network of 30,000 boys to sell his newspapers to small town customers across America.

William D. Boyce

Timing is everything. In 1909, Boyce was in the midst of a midlife crisis. He happened to be passing through London on his way to a South African adventure. He became disoriented crossing a street in the thick fog that enveloped London. A young man came out of the fog and offered to lead him. The young man refused to accept the tip Boyce offered, saying he was one of Baden-Powell's Boy Scouts and was doing his good turn for the day.

Baden-Powell said:

"[W]e encourage personal responsibility in the boy for his own physical development and health; and we trust in his honour and expect him to do a Good Turn to someone every day."

The name of that London Boy Scout is lost in history. At Gilwell Park, the English national Scouting Headquarters, there stands a large Silver Buffalo statue. It represents the Boy Scouts of America's Silver Buffalo Award for distinguished national service to Scouting. It is there in recognition of that unnamed Scout on a foggy London street in 1909 whose good turn got William Boyce interested in Boy Scouts. A plaque on the Silver Buffalo reads:

Whose faithfulness in the performance of the Daily Good Turn brought the Scout Movement to the United States of America.

Boyce was so impressed with a boy who would not accept a tip that he made an appointment to meet Baden-Powell. He and B-P discussed the Scouting program and how it could be brought to America.

At the time, there already were youth programs in America that had certain similarities to Scouting. In fact, B-P had borrowed heavily from the "Woodcraft" youth program that a naturalist named Ernest Thompson Seton (a British citizen living in America) had written down in a book called *Two Little Savages*. B-P reportedly used Seton's book as source material during his 1907 Brownsea Island experiment. However, Seton's books did not emphasize either youth leadership training or

Ernest Thompson Seton

the Patrol Method — the essential difference between Scouting and most other youth organizations.

Meanwhile, Daniel Beard had achieved fame by writing a best seller called *"The American Boys Handy Book: What to do and How to do it"* ("Let boys make their own kits and bows and arrows"). Beard founded an American youth organization called "Sons of Daniel Boone." He encouraged boys to form into "forts" and dress in buckskin. Beard's *"Handbook for the Boy Pioneers"* (written in 1909 — two years after Brownsea) was quite close to B-P's approach. However, Beard lacked the Patrol Method and the principles set forth in the Oath, Law, Motto and Slogan that Baden-Powell mixed into his own recipe for "Boy Scouting."

Seton, Beard and other passionate Americans soon became enthusiastic converts to Baden-Powell's Boy Scouting. Seton and Beard each saw advantages to the Boy Scout movement, and agreed to merge their organizations. Seton became Chief Scout of the United States when Boyce officially incorporated the Boy Scouts of America on February 8, 1910. Seton wrote the very first BSA Handbook for Boys by borrowing heavily from B-P's *Scouting for Boys*. Beard also contributed mightily to the effort to launch the BSA in America — serving as a National Commissioner for over thirty years.

Seton later came to believe the BSA was too militaristic. He thought the BSA's "Be Prepared" motto was a prescription for war. Seton repeatedly clashed with the BSA's first Scout Executive James E. West over future direction. Seton, who fundamentally remained a naturalist and a pacifist, once described West as "a man of great executive ability, but without knowledge of the activities of boys; who has no point of contact with boys, and who, I might almost say, has never seen the blue sky in his life." West fought back by claiming that Seton was an anarchist or radical socialist, and by smearing him for failing to become a U.S. citizen. West eventually forced Seton out of the BSA. West's refusal to allow Boyce to publish the BSA's official magazine also had the effect of channeling Boyce's efforts in other directions. However, Seton's Indian Lore work lives on in the BSA's Order of the Arrow, and Boyce went on to found the Lone Scouts of America ("LSA") that eventually merged with the BSA. "Uncle Dan" Beard remained an active contributor and BSA supporter for the rest of his life.

As we all know, the Boy Scouts of America went to become the largest Scouting organization in the world. The United States has had more Scouts than any other nation. BSA membership since 1910 totals more than 110 million. However, Scouting is worldwide. Since Baden-Powell's initiation of the program, some estimate that there have been 275 million Scouts across the world. There are currently 28 million Scouts worldwide in over 150 countries. Anyone who has been privileged to attend an International Jamboree knows how wonderfully diverse Scouting is around the world.

Scouting means many things to many people. However, our Scouts share Scouting Tradition, Scout Values and other important aspects of the Scouting Experience with millions of other Scouts in Europe, South America, Africa, Asia, Australia and other places all over the world. The World Brotherhood of Scouting is an important part of our Scouting tradition, and often has bridged the gap across international boundaries.

The Patrol Method is an essential aspect of the common heritage we all trace back to B-P's first experimental summer camp at Brownsea Island.

We should always remember "The Why" of Scouting. Without that understanding, we will fail B-P in our stewardship of the greatest youth program in the world today. A core ingredient of that program is the Patrol Method. The next section describes it from a Scoutmaster's perspective.

" Give full responsibility and show full confidence in your Patrol Leaders. Expect a great deal from them, and you will get it."

"The Patrol System is the one essential feature in which Scout training differs from that of all other organisations, and where the System is properly applied, it is absolutely bound to bring success. It cannot help itself!"

— Robert Baden-Powell

The Patrol Method:
A Scoutmaster's Perspective

Leadership Yarn 〜〜〜〜〜〜〜〜〜〜〜〜〜〜〜〜〜〜〜〜〜〜〜〜〜〜〜〜〜〜

The Shark Patrol volunteered to build the camp-fire for the Troop's Court of Honor. Tom, the Patrol Leader, called members of his Patrol a few days before the event and assigned tasks. John volunteered to bring tinder and matches. Owen said he would bring some wood. Michael offered to bring water, fire cans and a shovel. The whole Patrol agreed to arrive early and build the fire together.

When the Sharks arrived at the campfire site, they were surprised to find Assistant Scoutmaster Fitzpatrick already busy hauling logs to the fire ring. Mr. Fitzpatrick, an Eagle Scout, had thought of everything: tinder, matches, water cans, even a fire extinguisher.

"Guess we don't need these fire cans, huh Mr. Fitzpatrick?" asked Michael, looking down at the water cans he had just hauled in with much effort. "The more the merrier," said Fitzpatrick. "Just put them over there next to my jerry cans, we can use them all."

Fitzpatrick proceeded to "help" the Scouts construct the campfire. He put the largest logs in place himself, and made sure the tinder was well packed and strategically positioned. At one point, he rearranged some logs the Scouts had placed in the ring. "We want this to be right," said Fitzpatrick with a dash of authority. "The whole Troop will be watching."

Fitzpatrick was proud when the Shark's Patrol Leader lit the fire with a single match. "Some fire, huh?" he crowed to the parents around him, grinning ear to ear. Sure enough, the fire began to burn brightly and the flames stretched skyward. It was indeed an excellent campfire.

Fitzpatrick failed to see in the flickering firelight how he had deflated the Shark Patrol with his own superb efforts. He had taken away both their challenge and their chance to shine. By "helping" the Sharks, he had relieved them not only of the responsibility but also of the glory of building a great campfire. When

Fitzpatrick took over, the campfire was no longer the Shark's project — it became Fitzpatrick's project. Fitzpatrick stepped in and the Scouts backed away.

What Is the Patrol Method?

Scouts and Scouters hear and use the words "The Patrol Method" all the time. Surprisingly, few can articulate what it actually means or how to practice it. Typically, when we would ask Scouts to explain the Patrol Method during Scoutmaster Conferences, we would hear something about the "chain of command" or getting the guys to do what was needed. We would rarely hear an accurate description, even from Eagle Scout candidates.

> **Baden-Powell said:**
>
> "In all cases I would strongly commend the 'Patrol' system; that is, small permanent groups, each under responsible charge of a leading boy, as the great step to success."

Most Scouters know generally what the Patrol Method is, but they sometimes do not appreciate the central role of the Patrol Method in Scouting. Many do not seem to realize that the Patrol Method is *the* defining concept of the entire Scouting program — the "secret" to B-P's success at Brownsea Island.

Always Use the Patrol Method

The Patrol Method is essential to achieve the objectives of Scouting. If we are not using the Patrol Method, we are not following B-P's Scouting Way.

Leadership Yarn ꙮꙮꙮꙮꙮꙮꙮꙮꙮꙮꙮꙮꙮꙮꙮꙮꙮꙮꙮꙮꙮꙮꙮꙮꙮꙮꙮꙮꙮꙮꙮꙮꙮꙮ

The Bobcat Patrol of Troop 1137 was going on an overnight backpacking trip along the Appalachian Trail. The Patrol needed all of the following before hitting the trail:

- *transportation*
- *tour and park permits*

- *route planning*

- *maps*

- *schedule planning and emergency preparedness*

- *lightweight food*

- *water + water purification equipment/supplies*

- *Patrol equipment (tents, venturing tarp, first aid kit, backpacking stoves and fuel, lightweight cook kits, etc.)*

- *personal equipment.*

How can we arrange all this? In some Troops, a parent or Assistant Scoutmaster would just make it happen. However, Troop 1137 is Scout-led — it practiced the Patrol Method.

Joel, the Bobcat's Patrol Leader, asked the Bobcats to arrive 30 minutes before a Troop meeting so the Patrol could plan the backpacking trip. Joel came prepared with a list of things that the Patrol needed to take care of, and asked for volunteers.

Joe and Billy agreed to take care of buying the freeze-dried food and bringing the backpacking stoves and fuel — after the Patrol discussed and agreed on a menu.

Bobby agreed to be responsible for bringing the first aid kit and getting a topographic map and to bring his compass and GPS.

Jim and Tony volunteered to requisition enough lightweight tents for everyone from the Troop's Quartermaster.

George agreed to be responsible for bringing water purification tablets and equipment.

Everyone in the Patrol was responsible for something. All tasks were completed in a cooperative way.

If Patrol Leader Joel had tried to arrange all those details by himself, he would almost certainly have forgotten something. He did not yet have the organizational skills of an adult. Moreover, even if Joel were super-organized, he would probably end up making decisions that other members of his Patrol would not agree with. (For example, having freeze-dried tofu for dinner … ugh! … or deciding to sleep under a tarp even though the two 11-year-old Scouts in his Patrol needed the security of a tent). Some of the Patrol members would be unhappy. Some might even decide to stay home.

By calling a Patrol meeting before the backpacking trip, Joel was able to get the entire Patrol to invest in the idea of a backpacking overnighter. Some Patrol members needed a little persuading, but peer pressure can be a strong motivator. Besides, when the Patrol talked through the idea, it sounded like a lot of fun. No one wanted to miss that.

During the Patrol meeting, Joel asked for volunteers and assigned different tasks to different Scouts in the Patrol. The stage was set for a cooperative experience. Each participant had responsibility. Each participant invested in the endeavor. Everyone worked together towards a common goal.

The Patrol Method Defined

In Scouting, everything is done by Patrol. The Troop is important, but "The Patrol Rules!" During Troop meetings, the Scouts assemble by Patrol, sit by Patrol, play games by Patrol, and do all other activities by Patrol. On camping trips, Scouts travel, sleep, cook and eat by Patrol.

Baden-Powell said:

"The patrol is the unit of Scouting always, whether for work or for play, for discipline or for duty."

"My ideal camp is one where everybody is cheery and busy, where the Patrols are kept intact under all circumstances, and where every Patrol Leader and Scout takes a genuine pride in his camp ...."

The Patrol Method is what distinguishes Scouting from other youth groups. This basic leadership structure is the bedrock of our Scouting program.

Baden-Powell said:

"The Patrol System is the one essential feature in which Scout training differs from that of all other organisations, and where the System is properly applied, it is absolutely bound to bring success. It cannot help itself!"

When boys get together, they naturally form into smaller groups. Eventually, through group dynamics, one of them (usually older) ends up acting as a leader of sorts. Baden-Powell's genius was to realize that the basic tendency of boys to form into small groups could be used in the more formal organization of Scouting. Here is one simple way we sometimes explain the Patrol Method:

* A Patrol is a permanent group of five to eight Boy Scouts who work together as a team.

* Each Patrol is self-reliant and self-governing — that is, it operates independently (but is steered toward common goals by the Patrol Leaders Council and adult Troop leadership), decides what it wants to do and carries it out, takes care of itself, and is responsible for its own actions and performance.

* The Patrol is led by a Patrol Leader — an older Scout (not an adult) who is elected by his Patrol to lead and who is responsible, not just for himself — but also for the actions of the entire Patrol and for each Scout in the Patrol.

* The Patrol is the basic unit of Scouting. The Patrol sits together at meetings, camps together on campouts, works together on Troop fundraisers, and meets independently of the Troop to accomplish patrol goals. The Troop exists primarily to support the Patrols and to help coordinate activities involving multiple Patrols.

Baden-Powell said:

"The Patrol is the character school for the individual."

"To the Patrol Leader it gives practice in Responsibility and in the qualities of Leadership."

Give Your Patrol Leaders Real Authority

Life Scouts who sit for National Boards of Review before promotion to Eagle Scout are often asked, *"What is the most important leadership position in the Troop?"* It should come as no surprise that the correct answer is "Patrol Leader."

> **Baden-Powell said:**
>
> "Each Patrol Leader was given full responsibility for the behaviour of his patrol at all times, in camp and in the field."

It is the Patrol, not the Troop (as some people mistakenly think), that is the basic unit of Scouting. Therefore, the most important and critical leadership position in Scouting is Patrol Leader. He — and *only* he — carries the full, direct, "frontline" leadership responsibility for the Scouts in his Patrol.

> **Baden-Powell said:**
>
> "If the Scoutmaster gives his Patrol Leader real power, expects a great deal from him, and leaves him a free hand in carrying out his work, he will have done more for that boy's character expansion than any amount of school-training could ever do."

If there is only one thing in all of B-P's instruction that we Scoutmasters ought to put into practice, this is it!

Give Patrol Leaders real power. We should have the discipline and focus not to second-guess them, or to try to solve all their problems by telling them exactly what to do and how to do it. We should expect a great deal from them and train them so they are up to the task. We should then give them a free hand in carrying out their work and trust that they will do what they say they will do. We then sit back and watch.

Meanwhile, at the right time, we can mentor the Patrol Leader behind the scenes. We can give him feedback and pointers. However, when the Patrol is acting, let the Patrol Leader lead — we do not step in unless the situation presents a health or safety issue.

"We shouldn't undermine a Patrol Leader's leadership by talking down to him in front of others or by making it known that you as Scoutmaster are really the one in charge. Show your Patrol Leaders that you trust and respect them. Give them the authority to lead. Have faith in B-P's wisdom that the Patrol Method works. This is the true great mission of being a Scoutmaster."

— Rob Faris, Eagle Scout, Class of 1976

The Power, Privilege and Responsibility of Self-Governance

Most teenagers are constantly being told what to do and when to do it. Their teachers tell them what assignments to read and when to read them. Their parents tell them much more — everything from what to eat for dinner to when to be home from the dance to what school they should go to and what friends they should hang out with. Even strangers seem to have no problem correcting teen behavior.

B-P recognized that the Creator intended teenagers to experiment with independence and self-reliance. B-P also saw that often, such experiments were directed to non-constructive behavior that adults do not appreciate and which sometimes may even run afoul of the laws in our society (think of street gangs for example).

B-P's vision was to give boys lots of authority to make decisions and carry out actions. He intended that they do so within a structured, ethical framework offering defined objectives and the safety, guidance and wisdom of a watchful and involved Scoutmaster and his assistants.

This "adult association" aspect of the Scout program is much more than just boys and men hanging out together telling stories around a campfire. What B-P intended was that the Scoutmaster would channel the boys' objectives into constructive areas that would help develop citizenship and other life skills. In addition, he would do this by being involved and supportive while always observing Youth Protection, and by serving as an advisor with experience in common interest areas such as the outdoors.

A Patrol Leader position will likely give an average teenager more authority and responsibility than anything else he does at home or in school. Some boys are blessed with parents who give them appropriate degrees of independence. However, in many modern American homes, parents coddle their teenagers.

So-called "helicopter parents" are always ready to swoop down and save their children from failure, embarrassment or even hard work. The teens feel very safe and protected but are relatively powerless and often quite dependent.

As Scoutmasters, our mission is to give our Patrol Leaders the real power to lead, the authority and responsibility to make their own decisions in the context of an active and exciting outdoor program, and the credit for the outcome.

> *"There is no limit to what a man can do or where he can go if he doesn't mind who gets the credit."*
>
> — President Ronald Reagan

B-P envisioned that boys would practice this independent authority by deciding where and when to camp, how far to hike, what route to follow and what equipment to take. He wanted to replace antisocial behavior with constructive behavior.

Giving Scouts real power and control is important as a practical matter for retaining older Scouts in the program and getting their full participation in citizenship development and personal growth. A modern boy's life is often overfilled with activities. Adults will probably have planned most or all of these activities for him. School, after-school activities, sports, family activities — all of these are fun and useful but are mostly planned, organized and run by adults.

We can say to our Scouts, "This is your program. You decide what we will do." When do teachers or parents ask that question and actually mean it — without any strings attached? By entrusting the Scouts themselves with the power to control their own destinies within Scouting, we are offering them something they may not have received from any other activity involving adults.

With our adult skills and our adult connections, we are able to help the Patrol with transportation and other adult support that the Scouts would find difficult to arrange on their own. We also need to run interference to prevent parents or other well-meaning adults from stepping in and taking responsibility and authority away from the Patrol Leaders.

> *"The best leaders value their words, and use them sparingly. When he has accomplished his task, the people say, 'Amazing: we did it, all by ourselves!'"*
>
> — Tao Te Ching, by Lao-Tzu

Our mission is not to make sure the Troop's next weekend campout runs like clockwork — it is to train our Scouts to lead that weekend campout. Usually, the most difficult part of the Scoutmaster's mission is to structure the entire event appropriately so that responsibility remains with the Scouts and well-intentioned but untrained adults do not unwittingly sabotage the leadership-training mission.

Leadership Yarn

The Senior Patrol Leader asked John, a 15-year-old Star Scout who was not very sure of himself, to show new Scouts how to whip rope ends. John knew how to whip rope, but it had been awhile since he had demonstrated it so he was a little nervous. He began teaching the new Scouts gathered around him how to whip rope, but he was not teaching the skill particularly effectively. Some of the Scouts were just not getting it right away.

Suddenly, Mr. Michaels, the father of one of the new Scouts, stepped into the circle of Scouts with a rope and some twine. "Let me show you how they taught us in the Army," he said proudly and with an air of authority. Immediately, the new Scouts shifted their attention from John to Mr. Michaels. Mr. Michaels proceeded to show the new Scouts how to whip a rope "the Army way" — which happened to be different from the method taught in the Boy Scout Handbook. When John gently tried to point this out, Mr. Michaels verbally brushed him aside. "My way's quicker," Mr. Michaels said dismissively.

Mr. Michaels was proud to show off his ropework proficiency to his son and other new Scout friends. Mr. Michaels was so full of pride that he didn't notice as John, the 15-year-old Star Scout whom he had just summarily relieved, stepped back out of the circle, holding back tears of disappointment and frustration, and slowly walked away.

The most effective Scoutmasters encourage the Patrol Leaders Council to run the show. Through the Patrol Leaders Council and the individual patrol structure, Scoutmasters can challenge the boys to make things happen and then monitor the results, injecting themselves only when necessary. Now that is not to say we do not yell, "Don't touch that grill!" when we see a young Scout about to burn himself, or "Watch out with that ax" when we see a young Scout about to cut himself. However, it does mean that we try not to interfere when we see that the camp dinner is running late because someone did not get enough firewood.

Sometimes, negative experiential lessons help teach leadership and responsibility. In Scouting, we offer a "safe environment for failure" where the stakes are not that high. This strengthens the Scouts' resilience and gives them opportunities to see both success and failure because of their own efforts. Doing this in the outdoors makes the process immediate and effective.

> *"Never tell people how to do things. Tell them what to do and they will surprise you with their ingenuity."*
> — General George S. Patton, Jr.

But, what will the parents say about failures? Won't that reflect badly on the Scoutmaster? Not if we create the appropriate expectations from the beginning:

* Experienced Scoutmasters have a frank conversation with new Scout parents — usually before they formally register with the Troop.

* We explain to new parents that training leaders is a major goal of Scouting and our Troop.

* We tell them not to expect Troop events to run like a well-oiled machine.

* We tell them about the Patrol Method and how it works. We tell them they must have patience and understanding to allow it to work.

* We discuss that while adults have important roles and need to be very active in the Troop, they must not interfere with youth leadership opportunities.

* We try to create the expectation that when Scouts are leading other Scouts, the process may appear disorganized and inefficient but that the Scouts will eventually work through it and do it themselves.

Leadership Yarn

It had been raining all day at the Spring Camporee. It was up to the Lightning Bug Patrol to put up a tarp to shelter church services from the rain.

The Patrol had a huge nylon tarp. Lacking sufficient tarp poles, the older Scouts decided to tie the tarp to tree trunks. Some Scouts began climbing trees to tie ropes higher. Other Scouts were attempting to throw ropes into low hanging branches. The tarp was too large to visualize how to properly pitch it among the trees, and the readjustment of ropes in trees created an endless set of constantly changing variables. Some of the Scouts tied knots that failed. Some of the ropes slid down the tree trunks. Some of the Scouts were having trouble staying in the trees. The entire effort seemed as chaotic as it could be.

Yet, Patrol Leader Joel Hudson was in charge and leading the effort. He was directing Scouts to perform various tasks and evaluating the result. He was calling out requests and coordinating the team.

The time to begin church services was rapidly approaching, and the tarp was not yet up. Despite the loud ticking of his watch, Scoutmaster Bergen sat calmly in his chair, watching the leadership drama taking place around him. He did not offer unsolicited advice, nor did he begin barking orders.

Finally, with only a few minutes to spare, the tarp was up! Scoutmaster Bergen finally stood up from his chair, walked over to the Patrol Leader and said "Good job, Joel. That is a nice looking tarp. Go tell the Padre we're ready to proceed."

Patrol Leader Joel was on the top of the world — he had made a difference by leading his Patrol to provide shelter for the Camporee's church service.

Leadership Yarn

Mr. Paul, a retired military officer, was adult mentor for the Cougar Patrol of which his son was a member. Mr. Paul was an avid camper. He had all sorts of military surplus camping gear. He wanted to make sure the Cougars were the best equipped Patrol in the Troop, so he began bringing his own personal equipment to Troop campouts for the Cougars to use. The equipment was elaborate and complicated to set up, but Mr. Paul took pride in explaining to the Scouts how to set up the pop-up, how to rig the cook stove, and where to put everything so it was optimally configured.

One weekend, Scoutmaster Bergen happened by as the Cougars were setting up camp. Mr. Bergen watched as Mr. Paul directed everyone in the Cougar Patrol — including the Patrol Leader — on exactly what to do and in what order. That night, after the Scouts had gone to bed, Mr. Bergen and Mr. Paul were sipping coffee around the campfire.

"I was watching the Cougars set up camp this afternoon," said Mr. Bergen. "Pretty sweet setup."

Mr. Paul nodded with pride. "Yeah, I've been collecting that stuff for years," said Mr. Paul. "I'm glad the boys can get some use out of it."

"That gear is kind of complicated. How effective is the Patrol Leader in leading the boys to set it up?" Mr. Bergen asked.

"Hmm," thought Mr. Paul, who had an idea where the Scoutmaster was going. "The gear is kind of complicated. I figure so long as I keep my hands in my pockets and let the boys do everything, we're using the Patrol Method."

"Maybe," said Mr. Bergen. "But setting up camp is an important part of leadership training and teamwork. If you tell them all exactly what to do, then you're acting as the Patrol Leader."

Mr. Paul thought about it for a minute and the light bulb went on. "I guess you're right," he said sheepishly. "I'll bet the boys know how the equipment works now and can set it up on their own."

"Next time, you might try sitting in a camp chair and reading the newspaper. See what happens," Mr. Bergen suggested with a wry smile and a twinkle in his eye.

The last section was about what a Scoutmaster can do to structure an environment so the Patrol Method can flourish. The next section offers some ideas we have found useful to make the Patrol Method work better for the Scouts.

We have our Patrol Leaders take a Patrol Leaders Pledge following their election. It tends to focus them on their new office.

The Patrol Leader's Pledge

The Scouts of my Patrol have shown their confidence in me by electing me as their Patrol Leader. I understand this is more than an honor because it comes with great responsibility. I will live up to this responsibility by enthusiastically being the best Patrol Leader I can be. I pledge to lead my Patrol by my initiative and personal example and do each of the following to the best of my ability:

* **Regularly and enthusiastically attend** all Patrol and Troop meetings and activities.

* **Make a special effort to be a good friend** to each Scout in my Patrol and make each member of my Patrol know that I am personally interested in his rank advancement, his skill development and his training as a Scout.

* **Plan and carry out Patrol Activities** with my Scouts such as Patrol meetings, Patrol hikes, Patrol projects, Patrol Good Turns and other Patrol activities.

* **Keep well ahead of my Patrol in advancement and help my Scouts advance** in rank by training and examining them in Tenderfoot, Second Class and First Class requirements.

* **Promote strong Patrol pride and identity** by consistently using a Patrol name, a Patrol emblem and a Patrol cheer.

* **Train my Assistant Patrol Leader** and give each Scout in my Patrol a chance to do some leading in the Patrol.

* **Faithfully attend all PLC meetings** where I will represent my Patrol, do my part in helping to plan Troop events, bring before the Council the wishes of my Patrol, and take back to my Patrol the decisions of the Council.

* **Proudly wear my Scout uniform** to all Troop meetings and encourage my Scouts to do the same.

* **Live by the Scout Oath and Law and demonstrate Scout Spirit in everything I do.**

Patrol Member Rights and Responsibilities

* **Regularly and enthusiastically attend and participate** in all Patrol and Troop meetings and activities. I will let my Patrol Leader know in advance when I cannot attend.

* **Show all-for-one and one-for-all teamwork and attitude** and expect and encourage others in my patrol to do the same. I understand that my contributions to my Patrol make a difference and are important to my Patrol's effectiveness.

* **Make my thoughts and concerns known** to my Patrol Leader. Once my Patrol has voted on a course of action, I will be a good follower.

* **Do my best on advancement and skill learning** so I can strengthen my Patrol. I can and should expect my Patrol Leader to help me with my advancement.

* **Show Patrol Spirit** and be loyal to my Patrol. I am proud to be a member of my Patrol!

* **Do my best in my patrol office** and do some leading in my Patrol. If I am Assistant Patrol Leader, I will be prepared to take over when my Patrol Leader cannot attend or is busy doing something else.

* **Be true to Scouting** and wear my Scout uniform to Patrol and Troop functions.

* **Live by the Scout Oath and Law and demonstrate Scout Spirit in everything I do.**

Patrol Method: Building the Team

Leadership Yarn ⟿⟿⟿⟿⟿⟿⟿⟿⟿⟿⟿⟿⟿⟿⟿⟿⟿⟿⟿⟿⟿

The Condor Patrol was cooking dinner on a cool November campout. The long shadows showed that the sun would soon disappear behind the ridge. Larry, the Patrol's Grubmaster, had brought all the makings for chili and cobbler. Assistant Patrol Leader Luis had requisitioned two Dutch ovens from the Troop Quartermaster. The Condors had everything they needed to make a great dinner. The Patrol now needed to get a fire going to make hot coals, and get their dinner into the Dutch ovens. The Patrol was hungry and it was getting late.

Patrol Leader Tyrone wanted the Patrol to be done with the meal and cleaned up before dark. He knew he could save time if the tasks were divided up and done in parallel, so he formed his Patrol into small teams. He asked Luis and Mikey to build the fire, and he asked Larry and Jose to start mixing up the ingredients for the chili. Tom and Dave were already working on the cobbler (dessert was their favorite part of the meal). Tyrone would work with Luke to clean up after the meal.

Tyrone then noticed that Mikey was over on the other side of the campsite. He was just standing there away from everyone else and doing nothing at all. Tyrone's first thought was to yell at Mikey to get going.

Tyrone thought better of it. Instead of yelling in front of the Patrol, Tyrone walked over to Mikey and asked him if everything was all right. Mikey broke out in tears. Mikey complained that he was cold, tired and hungry. Tyrone could tell that Mikey was also homesick. Mikey was a new Scout. This was only his second campout.

Mikey had forgotten to bring a jacket, so Tyrone lent him an extra sweatshirt. Tyrone also gave Mikey a piece of a candy bar he had been saving. Tyrone knew the cure to homesickness was keeping busy, so he suggested that he and Mikey go out together and bring back wood. Tyrone told a few jokes while they worked.

By the time they got back to the campsite bearing armloads of fuel, Mikey had a big smile on his face. He could not wait to try out his new waterproof matches to start the fire. Tyrone suggested to Luis that he and Mikey should work together to lay the teepee fire but that it was Mikey's turn to light it. Soon Mikey and Luis had a fire blazing that cheered and warmed everyone.

Scoutmaster Pruit observed this interaction from an oak stump not far away. He just sat and watched. He made a mental note. Maybe the Patrol Leaders Council could benefit from some specialized discussions about how to make new Scouts more comfortable on their first camping trips away from home. Tyrone could lead that discussion. But, he thought, some of that discomfort is just a part of growing up and going through it with an older boy you look up to makes all the difference.

The Magic of Patrol Teamwork and Patrol Spirit

It is amazing what happens when six or eight Scouts get together in a Patrol — they form a team and start working together for the common good of the team. Each Scout wants to belong to the team and share in the activities of his team companions. They stand together, "All for one, and one for all!"

> **Baden-Powell said:**
>
> "It [the Patrol Method] teaches the boys to work together in teams. It secures co-operative effort for a common end; that is a democratic thing in and of itself."

It does not take long before the Scouts start thinking about the good of the whole team. The goals of the team become more important than the goals of individual Scouts.

> **Baden-Powell said:**
>
> "To the Scouts it [the Patrol Method] gives subordination of self to the interests of the whole, the elements of self-denial and self-control involved in the team spirit of cooperation and good comradeship."

A strong Patrol identity based on a distinctive Patrol name, cheer and flag leads to a healthy, friendly rivalry with other Patrols. With a little encouragement, each Patrol should want to be the best in the Troop. With healthy competition comes some learning.

The Patrol Method also creates synergy. Several people working together can accomplish more than one person trying to do it alone. Our Scouts often work on a big project such as building a pioneering tower, building steps on a trail for erosion control or collecting food for the poor. These are excellent opportunities for Scoutmasters to point out how Scouts working together as a team can accomplish a lot more than any Scout could accomplish by himself.

No one person can know everything. Combine six or eight individual sets of skills, experiences and capabilities in a Patrol and get a strong, well-rounded team.

For example, Joe might be a fire building wizard, Tom might be an orienteering expert, Scottie might love to cook, Jose might be a natural-born joke-teller, and Daryl might know lots about local animals and trees. The different skills and experiences of these boys complement one another. The Patrol Leader can use those skills collectively to accomplish Patrol objectives.

Through advancement and other activities, Scouts soon learn that they can rely on other members of their Patrol for help, advice and encouragement. Trust and cooperation begin to work hand in hand. Since Scouts spend most of their

Scouting time with their Patrols, the Scouting experiences they will probably remember the most will be with their Patrols.

The Patrol Leader's Work and Authority

Every Patrol needs a Patrol Leader. In American Scouting, the Scouts in the Patrol should elect their Patrol Leader. The Scoutmaster does not appoint Patrol Leaders. By electing their Patrol Leader, the Scouts in a Patrol are agreeing to give their Patrol Leader the authority to lead them. This is democracy in action at the grassroots level — and a unique opportunity for Scouts to govern themselves. By electing their Patrol Leader, the Scouts also agree to follow their Patrol Leader and serve as part of the team. For the same reason, electing Patrol Leaders from the Troop at large is usually much less effective than having each Patrol elect its own Patrol Leader.

Baden-Powell said:

"[A] Patrol Leader … [is elected] to responsible command of his Patrol. It is up to him to take hold of and to develop the qualities of each boy in his Patrol. It sounds a big order, but in practice it works."

A Patrol Leader is responsible for:

* himself,
* his Patrol overall, and
* each individual member of his Patrol.

A Scout who seeks the position of Patrol Leader must understand that in addition to being responsible for himself, he accepts responsibility for all actions of his Patrol. Most importantly (especially for a modern teenager), the Patrol Leader must understand that he is also accepting responsibility for each individual member of his Patrol. This is a tall order, but is extremely important for character development.

Leadership Yarn

After the Klondike Derby closing ceremony, each Patrol returned to its campsite to pack up and break camp. Someone soon noticed that Scout Jeff Thompson was missing. Scoutmaster Bergen asked Jim, the missing Scout's Patrol Leader, "Where is Scout Jeff?"

"I don't know," Jim said. "He's always wandering off."

"You're responsible Jim, you had better go look for him," Scoutmaster Bergen replied.

Jim was not exactly pleased to be told that he was responsible for the whereabouts of this wayward 11-year-old. It had never dawned on Jim until that moment that he was actually responsible for the health, safety, well-being and conduct of this young tenderfoot Scout. After all, it was a big responsibility. Jim could be having much more fun hanging out with buddies his own age than worrying about Tenderfeet. However, he soon understood that caring and being responsible for others comes with the territory of leadership.

For the Patrol to function effectively and efficiently, it has to be led. The Patrol Method is the means by which the Patrol operates. It is the Patrol Leader's job to make that happen through his good leadership. An added benefit of dividing the Troop up into small, manageable teams is the creation of more leadership positions. This gives more Scouts a chance to lead.

Forming the Patrol

How can a Patrol Leader get six or eight Scouts of different ages and experiences to form a Patrol and work together as a team? There seems to be three basic steps:

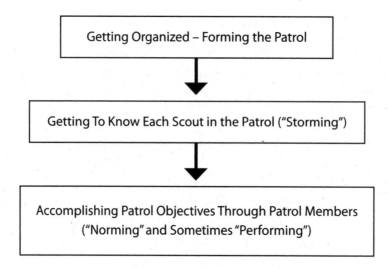

So a leader can adjust leadership styles based on group dynamics, it is important for the leader to recognize where the team is in this successive process. Educational psychologists have defined four separate stages of team building:

Stage I. "Forming" (Courteous Caution): Scouts want to be accepted by other Scouts and so are on their best behavior, but they also tend to perform independently and are very focused on themselves. The Patrol therefore focuses on being busy with routines and organization. During this stage, the Scouts are also gathering information and impressions about each other. This stage is a great time to make new friends. The "Forming" stage is comfortable, but the desire to avoid conflict means that not much gets done and confusion usually reigns.

Stage II. "Storming" (Conflicting Chaos): Patrol members open up to each other and confront each other's ideas and perspectives. As important issues arise, some Scouts' patience will break and minor confrontations will occur. Immature Patrol members will begin trying to show off how much they know to convince others that their ideas are correct. Storming can be contentious, unpleasant and even painful to Scouts who don't like conflict. Tolerance and respect need to be emphasized. Depending on the maturity of the Patrol members, a Patrol may never move out of the Storming phase — or it may continually revert to it when presented with new challenges. The Patrol Leader needs to be very directive and demonstrative in his leadership style to bring his Patrol through the storms.

Stage III. "Norming" (Collaboration): The Patrol agrees on rules and methods. Patrol members begin to trust one another. Patrol members begin to appreciate one another's skills and experiences. Individuals listen to one other. They begin to appreciate and support each other. They feel they are part of a cohesive, effective group. Motivation increases. Since the Patrol has worked hard to get to this stage, it may resist any pressure to change (especially from the outside) out of fear it will regress back to "Storming."

Stage IV. "Performing" (Trusting Creativity): Not all Patrols reach this final stage. It provides stability, interdependence and flexibility. The Scouts now know one another well enough to work together effectively and efficiently. They trust one another enough to allow independent activity. Members are motivated and knowledgeable. They are considerate of one another and respect one another. Roles and responsibilities change according to need in an almost seamless way. There is strong group identity, strong group loyalty and high morale. The team solves problems in creative ways that maximize use of team resources. Dissent is expected and is handled respectfully in a way that is acceptable to the entire team. All of the energy of the Patrol can be directed towards the tasks at hand. All for one and one for all!

Patrols need concentrated effort and well defined goals to proceed through these stages. In some Troops, Patrols never progress beyond the Forming or Storming stages. Intense team exercises such as Patrol Cooking, Patrol Pioneering and inter-Patrol competition can allow a Patrol to move to Norming or even Performing. Constantly introducing new members into the Patrol or shuffling Patrol members around will almost guarantee that the Patrol will constantly regress back to Storming or even Forming.

Patrol Identity

To prevent regression and encourage collaboration and team spirit, each Patrol should have a distinct identity — a name, a logo, a cheer, and a patch, emblem or totem. This might seem optional or useful primarily for logistical purposes, but it goes to the heart of Patrol spirit. When a Patrol has worked together for a while, the members of that Patrol each identify themselves as a member of that Patrol. Because of Patrol Spirit, they become an Owl, a Bear, a Bobcat or maybe a Viking. They are proud to be a member of that Patrol. They belong. They are happiest when working together as a Patrol team.

Many Troops long ago decided how many Patrols to have. B-P recommended that the Patrols become permanent. For example, there might always be Bears, Wildcats, Panthers, and so forth. Some modern American Scout Patrols tend to like to decide (and change) their Patrol Name based on shared experiences along the Scouting trail. Patrol name aside, an advantage of designating permanent Patrols is that they develop a legacy. New Scouts assigned to a Patrol with more senior Scouts can stay in the same Patrol until they themselves become senior Scouts. Shuffling members between Patrols is usually a bad idea — it tends to weaken team spirit and identity.

At the beginning of the Scouting year, each Patrol should:

* Decide on a Patrol vision

* Set specific Patrol Goals that meet the SMART test (Specific, Measurable, Attainable, Relevant & Timely)

* Set a Patrol meeting schedule

* Elect officers within the Patrol (after the Patrol Leader appoints his Assistant Patrol Leader) such as a Scribe, Grubmaster, Scout Spiritmaster, and Quartermaster

* Set up an email or telephone tree for communications

* Identify skill sets of each Scout (e.g., cooking, fire building, knot-tying, orienteering, first aid, etc.)

* Develop personal advancement plans for each Patrol member

* Schedule Patrol activities such as hikes, service projects and camping trips

- Come up with a list of proposed Troop activities the Patrol Leader should push for when the Patrol Leaders Council meets to plan the Troop calendar

- Identify any needed equipment, books or other resources

- Consider asking a parent of one of the Patrol members or one of the Troop's Assistant Scoutmasters to be a Patrol Mentor. *[Important: the adult Patrol mentor is **not** equivalent in any way to a Cub Scout Den Leader — this adult should be well trained **not** to undercut the Patrol Leader's leadership.]*

The Troop gets lots of attention in modern Scouting. In some Troops, Patrols do not do much of anything as Patrols. In such Troops, the Patrols get together only during "Patrol Corners" at Troop meetings and the Troop organizes all activities. It should not be that way. Baden-Powell designed Scouting with the Patrol as the basic unit of Scouting. Patrols must always support and be loyal to the Troop, but "the Patrol Rules!"

We Scoutmasters should expect Patrols to meet and have their own individual activities now and then. Maybe they will meet just for some advancement skills and then eat pizza or shoot baskets in the driveway. Or perhaps Patrols that are more ambitious will have their own campouts, hikes or other trips. How about a Patrol model rocketry day? What about a Patrol Good Turn? Or a Patrol hike? When Patrols get out there and do things as a Patrol, the result will likely be some very interesting competitions and a much stronger Troop.

A Troop is only as strong as its weakest Patrol. Scoutmasters should mentor the Senior Patrol Leader to work with each Patrol Leader to help make each Patrol strong. If the Patrols are strong, the Troop will also be strong. The way to strengthen a Patrol is to have the Patrol work together as a team as much as possible.

Modern American boys are often overscheduled. How can a modern Patrol run effectively when its members don't show up for activities due to scheduling conflicts? An ideal solution is for Patrol members to be so dedicated to their Patrol that they don't want to miss any Patrol activity. We have seen Patrol Spirit strong enough to overcome most scheduling conflicts. Nevertheless, what does a Patrol Leader do, as a practical matter, when half his Patrol does not show up for a Troop event? Some Troops pair Patrols permanently together so that two Patrols can form a single combined Patrol when necessary. This can weaken the Patrol structure but is preferable to staying home. Another way: form large

Patrols so each Patrol can still function as a team even if scheduling conflicts prevent some members from attending a particular event.

Leading the Individual: Learning about Each Patrol Member

We tell our Patrol Leaders they must get to know each member of their team. The same is true for the Scoutmaster and other adult leaders. The more we Scoutmasters know about each Scout in our Troop, the better we are able to train them to lead.

The Scoutmaster needs to know each Scout in the Troop but he needs to know a bit more about the Scouts on the Patrol Leaders Council. Senior Patrol Leaders should know their Patrol Leaders very well. Patrol Leaders should know each member of their Patrols. To lead a group means leading each member of the group. This often requires the leader to give individual attention to each member of the group.

Leaders, adult and Scout, need to know more than the name of each Scout. They need to know the person — his motivations, his likes/dislikes, his concerns, his interests, the way he interacts with others, his maturity level, his physical capabilities, and other aspects of his personality. It is critical for a Patrol Leader to know a lot about each member of his Patrol. Senior Patrol Leaders and Scoutmasters can foster this approach.

Understand the Characteristics and Needs of Your Team and Each Team Member

"I used to tell leaders in my units, both enlisted and officer, that to be an effective leader you must do three things and do them well:

1. *Lead from the Front: Share the same hardships as your followers.*

2. *Set the Example: Live the Army values. Do the hard right over the easy wrong.*

3. *Take Care of Your Soldiers. Know them. Know their likes and dislikes. Know what makes them tick. Train them to be able to do your job.*

I also told them that if they were good leaders, the first two should come easy but the third one was the hardest — but that it was our responsibility as leaders to take care of our soldiers in everything we did."

— Command Sergeant Major Harry Wimbrough (retired),
Third United States Infantry Regiment ("The Old Guard")
Eagle Scout Class of 1975 and U.S. Army Ranger

Leaders need to take time to know each Scout because it helps build trust and friendships as well as respect. As Scoutmasters, we lead our Troop most effectively through mutual trusting relationships with each Scout — especially those on the Patrol Leaders Council. We want the Scouts to trust us, but we also need to trust our Scouts. The same is true of Patrol Leaders. However, building trusting, friendly relationships takes time and attention. It requires working closely over time with those whom we lead.

Baden-Powell said:

"Men talk of having fine Troops of 60 or even 100 — and their leaders tell me that their boys are equally well trained as in smaller Troops. I express admiration ('admiration' literally translated means 'surprise') and I don't believe them. 'Why worry about individual training?' they ask. Because it is the only way by which you can educate. You can instruct any number of boys, a thousand at a time if you have a loud voice and attractive methods of disciplinary means. But that is not training — it is not education."

We find it is useful as adults to try to meet each Scout's parents and get to know them a bit, too. Our goal as leaders is to understand who each Scout is and become their trusted colleague. That sort of caring individual attention will forge a bond of trust and loyalty that strengthens leadership.

"There's a great deal of talk about loyalty from the bottom to the top. Loyalty from the top down is even more necessary and is much less prevalent. One of the most frequently noted characteristics of great men who have remained great is loyalty to their subordinates."

— General George S. Patton, Jr.

"Loyalty is not blind faith. If you see a leader doing something wrong, a loyal person would tell him so. True loyalty requires that you sometimes bear bad tidings."

— Ted Knight, Eagle Class of 1962

If a Patrol Leader knows a lot about each individual member of the team, he also will know a lot about the team overall. Patrol Leaders need to know that their most valuable resources are the Scouts in their Patrol. Likewise, a Scoutmaster's most valuable resources are the leaders in the Patrol Leaders Council and the adults who work with us.

Scoutmasters work through their Scouts to get things done. That means we have to be continually certain that the older Scouts are teaching the younger ones a wide range of skills including leadership skills. This will help get the job done faster and better. It will help us to better understand what the team can and cannot do and when we might need to get help from other resources. Most importantly, it will help us to develop future leaders.

Know and Use Your Team Resources

Leadership Yarn

The Wildcat Patrol was competing in an inter-Patrol pioneering competition at the District Camporee. The competition tested teamwork — the Wildcats had to work together to have a chance at winning.

Joe, the Patrol Leader, gave each Scout an assignment. He explained why each assignment was important to the overall task. Some Scouts needed to hold the spars in position so other Scouts could work the ropes and tie lashings.

To make the right assignments, Joe needed to know the pioneering skills of each Scout in the Patrol. Two of the Scouts, Jose and Nick, were expert lashers — in fact, they both earned Pioneering Merit Badge at summer camp. Joe was wise to ask them to tie the square lashings since he knew of their expertise. If Joe did not know ahead of time, he might have needed to ask some questions or come up with an exercise to learn which Scouts knew how to lash best.

Scoutmaster Sandoval also knew from watching recent First Class advancement instruction that Adam knew his shear lashing pretty well but did not yet have much confidence. If the Patrol Leader failed to recognize this, it might be appropriate for the Scoutmaster to pull him aside and respectfully suggest that he might ask Adam to tie one of the shear lashings. Even though Adam would be nervous about doing it, he was probably going to do all right and he would feel like a hero by using his new skill for the good of the Patrol.

Baden-Powell said:

"Each boy in the Patrol realises that he is in himself a responsible unit and that the honour of his group depends in some degree on his own ability in playing the game."

As leaders, we need to remember that we too are team resources. Scoutmasters are very important resources to their Scouts. To be effective resources, we need to be honest with ourselves about our own capabilities. Do not be afraid to give other adults and Scouts a chance to shine. After all, another characteristic of a good leader is the ability to find the right resources to get the job done. If a Patrol Leader, Senior Patrol Leader or Scoutmaster does everything just because he can or knows how to, he is leading only one person — himself.

If we have an orienteering expert among the adults, we ask him to be in charge of mentoring Patrol instruction on orienteering. If we have a fellow who loves to cook and does a great job at it, we give him responsibility for adult meals. Using these resources does not challenge leadership — to the contrary, it shows that a good leader uses his resources wisely and efficiently.

We try to figure out what makes each Scout and adult tick. What puts a smile on his face? What makes him proud? What are his goals and interests? What is his family like? Get him to open up. Try to establish trust. Try different approaches to see what works. Keep in mind that everyone wants to belong and everyone wants to feel important. The leader's job, at all levels, is to give each group member both opportunities.

It may take some time to figure out the right way to handle certain Scouts. Praise often works wonders — usually, so does explaining "The Why." We have found that an effective way to get some of the "problem" Scouts in line is to give them real responsibility. The guy who is always criticizing the best efforts of everyone else is not going to criticize a result if he was in charge and feels some ownership. The less motivated (or even lazy) Scout cannot just sit there and do nothing if he is responsible for getting a job done. Sharing strengthens leadership.

Control Undesirable Behavior

Baden-Powell taught us to hold Patrol Leaders responsible for what goes on among the boys of their Patrols. This means that in a Scout-led Troop, the Scouts themselves should be primarily responsible for disciplining. Scoutmasters may sometimes need to step in, but think it through carefully before you intervene. Do the Scouts need help to deal with this problem? Are you undermining the authority of your boy leaders by stepping in? Is there a less intrusive way for you to accomplish what you need to accomplish? For example, can you pull the offending Scout aside for a private talk? Should you get the Scout's Patrol Leader involved? Start by training your boy leaders to discipline effectively without hazing or dangerous use of isolating techniques. Once trained, they may be able to accomplish more with peer pressure than you could ever accomplish with adult authority.

Leadership Yarn ～～～～～～～～～～～～～～～～～～～～～～～～～～～～～～

Assistant Scoutmaster Rogers was frustrated. Flag ceremony was in fifteen minutes and most of the Scouts were not yet in uniform. The evening before, one patrol showed up to camp assembly late and not in uniform. Rogers was not about to let that happen again — not on his watch.

"Everyone assemble right now!" Rogers boomed across the campsite. "I don't care what you're doing, drop it and form up." As the Troop assembled, Senior Patrol Leader Tom Evans looked expectantly at Mr. Rogers for a cue. Rogers brushed the SPL aside, and began a tirade. He dressed the Troop down for making him personally look bad in front of the rest of the camp. "I always manage to get into my uniform. What's wrong with you?" he asked a disorganized Tenderfoot Scout who was still in his bathing suit, bringing the Scout close to tears. Rogers proceeded to ridicule a few other Scouts individually, and then told the Troop he wanted to see

them all back in seven minutes in full uniforms. SPL Evans stood on the sidelines, feeling totally ineffective and bad about failing his Scoutmaster.

Rogers accomplished his goal of getting all Scouts in uniform, but the way he went about it destroyed the confidence of his leaders and served only to demonstrate that he (Rogers) was actually the (only) one in charge. Proper uniforming is not a health and safety issue. Motivating Scouts to get into uniform is something Patrol Leaders and Senior Patrol Leaders are perfectly capable of handling. Rogers made a mistake by grabbing for himself the authority to correct the problem. He bypassed his Senior Patrol Leader and Patrol Leaders in the process. There were less intrusive ways for Rogers to accomplish the objective. How about asking the Senior Patrol Leader to call for a uniform inspection? If each Patrol Leader had to orally report to the SPL in front of the rest of the assembled Troop, the offending Scouts would probably immediately correct their uniforming problems.

Motivational Leadership

Discipline and participation problems will occur in every active Scout Troop. Sometimes it is best to ignore a Scout's antics. Often we can use the rest of the group to exert peer pressure on a Scout. Other times a lighter, individual touch is the more effective approach. Think of different motivational techniques as tools in a toolbox — try to select just the right tool for the job at hand. Different tools work best with different people and different problems.

Some Motivational Tools:

* Delegate — Ownership will often turn a lazy Scout into a productive Scout
* Praise — Sharing Credit
* Explaining "The Why"
* "I Need Your Help"
* Peer Pressure — Belonging
* Humor
* Understanding — walk in the other person's boots
* Trust

Leadership Yarn ～～～～～～～～～～～～～～～～～～～～～～～～～～～～～～～～～

The Patrol Leaders Council convened at the local burger joint to discuss the up-coming whitewater rafting trip. All Patrols were represented except for the Eagles. Jack, the Patrol Leader of the Eagles, was not there. Jack was not carrying his share of the load. He was not coming to Troop meetings or outings, and now he was missing Patrol Leaders Council meetings. His Patrol was continually "out of the loop" and on outings was often leaderless.

Jack's absence did not go unnoticed. Scoutmaster Jones did not want to make an example of Jack, but he knew something had to be done. He decided he should talk to Jack's parents and to Jack himself. However, without Scoutmaster Jones saying a word about it, the Scouts in the Patrol Leaders Council raised the issue on their own. After dscussion, the PLC's consensus was that Jack was not doing his best.

The Patrol Leaders Council decided that the Senior Patrol Leader and his assistant would meet with Jack during the next Troop meeting to discuss the problem. The decision came from among Jack's peers and the action was reasonable. Scoutmaster Jones did not become involved except to monitor the interaction and be certain the PLC handled it in a constructive manner.

During the next Troop meeting, the Senior Patrol Leader and his ASPL took Jack aside. The Scoutmaster observed from the other side of the meeting room. The discussion was respectful but firm and constructive.

Jack was hurt at being "found out" but he was also relieved not to have to maintain the charade. He knew he was not being an effective Patrol Leader. His lacrosse schedule conflicted with Troop meetings, and he had been choosing lacrosse over Scouts. He also recognized that he needed more training in what to do as a Patrol Leader.

Jack agreed to attend some of the Troop's leadership training sessions, and said he would think about a weeklong National Youth Leadership Training session in the summer. Meanwhile, he agreed to step back from the Patrol Leader position and ask his Patrol to elect a new leader who could come to all the meetings. He could run again for the office in the next election.

Scouting Is Not "Pass/Fail"

Mistakenly, parents and Scouts often view Scouting as a "pass/fail" situation. Ever notice how new Scout parents ask "does this count?" when trying to obtain credit for skills their son has demonstrated away from the eyes of his Patrol

Leader? They seem to regard Scouting as similar to schoolwork and grades — with a list of advancement requirements to check off (the sooner the better). That is completely wrong for so many reasons.

In Scouting, we offer a safety net to failure. *A Scout can try and fail without any major consequences or retribution.* We try to make each effort a learning experience by which the Scout continually improves. We provide a foundation for those efforts with the application of the Patrol Method and the principles of our program as embodied in the Scout Oath, Law, Motto and Slogan.

Most Scouts have seven years from enrollment to their 18th birthday to achieve all requirements for Eagle Scout. No Scout has to do them all in the first two or three years. It is more important that Scouts learn to do them right even if it takes seven years. It is our job to provide the structure so our Scouts can do just that — learn Scout skills and leadership the correct way.

> "Scouting is not an achievement or yet another item to add to your college application — it's a way of life. A Scout is best served taking the full seven years of his youth between 11 and 18 to advance toward Eagle and practice the leadership lessons of Scouting. After that, he can give a lifetime of service. Once an Eagle, always an Eagle."
>
> — Ted Knight, Eagle Class of 1962

Leadership Yarn

Scout Don James was a merit badge dynamo. His parents did not push Don into it — Don was intellectually curious and interested in every topic under the sun and was very achievement oriented.

Early in his Scout career, Don had embarked on an ambitious plan to earn so many merit badges that they would overflow onto the backside of his sash. He earned Electricity and Electronics, Sheep Raising and Snow Sports, Law and Pioneering, Basketry and Plumbing, Insect Life and Mammals — more and more. At summer camp, his merit badge schedule was a full as it could be. He ran from one activity station to another, attending class after class.

In earning all those merit badges, Don was not necessarily concentrating on the Eagle required ones. By his 16th birthday, Don had earned over 40 merit badges but still had not begun Emergency Preparedness or Lifesaving, Personal Fitness and a few other Eagle-required badges.

One evening at summer camp, Scoutmaster Wong saw Don sitting at a picnic table, busily writing up yet another merit badge requirement. Scoutmaster Wong sat down at the table and complimented Don on his work ethic and merit badge achievements. Don got a big smile on his face (Don aimed to please). Wong then told Don that when he (the Scoutmaster) had received his own Eagle Award, he had earned exactly 21 merit badges — no more and no less.

Don stopped writing and looked up. That was a new concept for him — in fact, it sounded to Don like an embarrassing admission. "Why?" asked Don. "There are so many other interesting merit badges."

Scoutmaster Wong looked directly at Don for effect: "It took me a long time to earn those 21 merit badges. I wanted to make sure I knew each required badge inside and out. First Aid and Lifesaving skills can help you save someone's life, so I worked especially hard on those. I spent the rest of my time working on outdoor and leadership skills. I taught the younger Scouts how to start fires, how to tie lashings, and some other advanced stuff like land navigation and baking in clay ovens you build yourself."

At this point, Don had put his pencil down. His Scoutmaster now had Don's full attention. "But you don't get any credit for all of that," said Don. "I'm being a leader by earning all these badges."

As always, Scoutmaster Wong was candid and direct: "No, Don, you're not. You are demonstrating that you can motivate yourself to do wonderful things. That very valuable skill will serve you well in life. However, in earning all these badges, you are not leading or teaching anyone other than yourself. While you're off working on all these merit badges, you're not available to the new Scouts who could really use your help and experience."

This was the first of several conversations between Don and his Scoutmaster. Don completed all the merit badges he had signed up for at camp that summer, but in the Fall, he focused on required badges and on his Eagle leadership project. He also took on more major Troop leadership responsibilities, and became the Troop firebuilding instructor.

Don never did complete enough badges to overflow onto the backside of his sash, but he was not disappointed. Scoutmaster Wong got him to understand that the Eagle medal on his chest and the leadership bars on his shoulder meant far more *than the self-absorbed glamour of an oversized array of brightly colored circles on his merit badge sash.*

Control Team Performance

A leader must help while controlling the overall process and the performance of the entire team. He must also evaluate the team and its progress as the process is evolving. He needs to make decisions "on the fly" to achieve the best results — just like the captain of a ship must make course corrections from time to time. He must not be afraid to correct poor performance. However, he should keep a positive attitude to motivate team members to do their best and work together. A Scoutmaster should be especially careful to avoid micromanaging. Give Patrol Leaders real authority to make their own decisions and their own mistakes. Encourage them to use the Start/Stop/Continue evaluation tool (what should I start doing that I'm not already doing? What should I stop doing? What should I continue doing because it's working?)

> *"Improvise, Adapt and Overcome."*
> — Unofficial mantra of the United States Marine Corps.

Here is one good way Scouts can work together using the Patrol Method:

* The Patrol Leader, after discussion with his Patrol, identifies a goal — for example, going on a camping trip, completing a particular advancement skill or doing a Patrol service project.

* The Patrol Leader decides on an overall plan of action and does his homework by coming up with a detailed set of manageable steps to accomplish the goal.

* The Patrol Leader identifies particular skills needed to carry out each step of the action plan.

* The Patrol Leader determines whether members of the Patrol have the needed skills and if not, how to make those skills available (for example, by teaching those skills or finding a "how to" book in the Troop Library).

* The Patrol Leader assigns the various tasks to different Patrol members and schedules the work.

- The Patrol reviews the plan and agrees with it (this is important if Patrol members are to take ownership).

- The Patrol works together to carry out the plan (the Patrol Leader is responsible for controlling the performance of the entire team).

- During and after execution, the Patrol continually evaluates how it did and discusses what it could have done better (i.e., Start/Stop/Continue, and "Roses and Thorns" type discussions).

This section has presented some suggestions we have found helpful in making the Patrol Method work for our Scouts. We hope you will find them useful as well. The next section focuses on what it means to do one's best. B-P was a wise fellow. He did not charge us with the impossible — being perfect — but he did challenge us to do our best. The next section explores what that means.

Striving for Excellence: Doing Your Best

Baden-Powell did not set standards that were impossible for us to achieve. Our Oath does not say, "succeed at all costs" or "do the absolute best." B-P knew we are not perfect, but he wanted us to take responsibility to strive for excellence. Therefore, that is the next leadership lesson:

"On My Honor, I Will Do My Best"

If we do not do our best, we short-change our fellow Scouts and ourselves. No Scout is perfect. However, when a Scout does not do his best, problems can come up and deep down inside he knows he failed — not necessarily at the task — but at doing his best.

Leadership Yarn 〰〰〰〰〰〰〰〰〰〰〰〰〰〰〰〰〰〰〰〰〰〰〰〰〰〰

The Wildcats were enjoying their first hike of the season. It was a perfect Fall day, and everyone was having a great time. Everyone, that is, except for Tenderfoot Scout Johnny Milner. Johnny was dead last on the trail. He could not seem to keep up.

Charlie, the Wildcat's Patrol Leader, was out in front. He looked back and noticed the delay. "Come on Johnny, let's get going!" Charlie yelled back down the trail. "I want our Patrol to get to camp first!"

Johnny grunted and tried to walk a little faster but any-one could see he was having trouble — if anyone had been paying attention. Johnny had made the mistake of wearing brand new boots that he had not yet broken in. Now, several miles into the hike, every step was torture.

Half an hour later, Charlie led five of the Wildcats into camp. They all took off their daypacks, plopped down under a tree and began eating lunch. The rest of the Patrol including Johnny arrived some time later. By this time, Johnny was hobbling so badly that he could barely stand. He sat down and took off his right boot. Everyone stared at a huge crop of red puffy blisters.

Charlie started feeling bad. He realized how he had let this young Tenderfoot down. Charlie had been carrying moleskin in his daypack all along and knew how important blister treatment was, but he had never even offered to help Johnny. He had not even noticed that Johnny was having trouble. Charlie had been so anxious to beat the other Patrols into camp that he had totally ignored the well-being of one of his Patrol members.

Doing *your best* is a very personal matter. The Scout Oath says "Do *My* Best" — not "Do *the* Best." No one but the individual Scout will know whether he did his personal best. Others can tell if he succeeded or failed at the task, but they cannot really know whether he put out his personal best effort.

So we ask our Scouts, "what does it mean to do your best?"

Doing your best means working to the best of your abilities. It means giving it your all … and living up to (and sometimes exceeding) your own expectations of what you are capable of. It means being true to yourself.

Doing your best is taking your knowledge and skills and all the other resources available to you, and putting them to work the best way you know how to solve a problem or make a situation better.

It is an important measure of a leader who, when faced with a challenge — especially an unexpected one — can do his best to overcome obstacles and adapt to meet the challenge head-on to the best of his ability.

Life teaches us that doing our best does not always guarantee success. Matching visions and dreams with goals is not easy. Even applying the most useful goal-setting tool, the goal may be too ambitious. Maybe the right resources are not available. Sometimes, achieving the goal was just not meant to be — it cannot be accomplished no matter how hard you try. Sometimes a leader may find he has not yet developed the necessary skills or does not yet have enough experience. However, if a Scout truly does his best, he may sometimes be disappointed in the result but he will never be disappointed in himself. Scouts need to know this.

Baden-Powell said:

"It is the satisfaction of having successfully faced difficulties and borne pin-pricks that gives completeness to the pleasure of having overcome them. Don't expect your life to be a bed of roses; there would be no fun in it if it were."

"Just as fire tempers iron into fine steel, so does adversity temper one's character into firmness, tolerance and determination."

— Sen. Margaret Chase Smith, Lt. Col. USAF Reserve

Leaders must set the expectation for others to do their best. In modern American society, teenagers or their parents sometimes translate "do your best" into "with Mom or Dad's help." We have met some Life Scouts whose Mom or Dad was actually somehow behind nearly every merit badge on the sash. Resisting this approach in favor of Scout self-reliance, self-achievement and self-responsibility is a constant vigil.

Leadership Yarn

Not yet thirteen years old, Scout Ian Morrison had already received 25 merit badges and was now asking the District to approve his highly ambitious Eagle Leadership project. Was this boy a prodigy, or was there some other explanation?

Mr. Robins, the District Eagle representative, sat down with Ian and his father to review the young Scout's project write-up and other Scouting credentials. "Young man, you have received a lot of merit badges in your short time in the Scouts. You must really love Scouting!" commented Mr. Robins enthusiastically.

"Yes, he does" Ian's father, Mr. Morrison, answered for Ian with pride in his voice.

"I have read your project write-up and I think it's quite good … maybe too good" said Mr. Robins, looking at Mr. Morrison for effect.

"What do you mean 'too good'?" asked Mr. Morrison defensively.

Mr. Robins ignored Mr. Morrison's question and turned to Scout Ian. "Ian, did you write this?"

Ian spoke for the first time. "No, my Dad wrote it for me," he said truthfully.

"I thought so," Mr. Robins said flatly.

Mr. Morrison interrupted before his son could say anything else. "So what if I wrote it," he thundered. "It's still his project."

Mr. Robins sat back in his chair and looked at Mr. Morrison for a few seconds. Then he turned to Ian. "Ian, I think you had better excuse us for a few minutes. Your Dad and I have some things to talk about privately. My son Jerry is watching television in the den. Why don't you go visit with him?""

After Ian had left the room, Mr. Robins calmly and firmly told Mr. Morrison that he had noticed how Mr. Morrison had signed off on all 25 of his son's merit badges. Also, some of the sign-off dates did not make any sense (for example, the records showed his boy had supposedly completed Personal Fitness and Personal Management only a few days after he began working on those badges).

Mr. Robins took off his glasses, wiped them and looked earnestly at Mr. Morrison. "Mr. Morrison, your son may make a fine Eagle Scout someday, but he's not ready yet. I will not approve this project. It is excessively ambitious for a 12 year old. He does not yet have the skills. He will learn only the wrong things if you do the project for him. You need to wait until your boy is ready to come up with his own project."

There are of course instances in which adult assistance or mentoring is highly appropriate. However, we adult leaders need to be sensitive to each Scout's capabilities. A Scout may actually be doing his best even though he seems to be falling behind everyone else. The next yarn tells of a very special Scout of our acquaintance.

Leadership Yarn

Over 100 people attended the 18-year-old's Eagle ceremony at the United Methodist Church. It was the most moving and inspirational Eagle ceremony in recent memory.

This Eagle presentation was special. George Rogers, the young man receiving the Eagle badge, had Down syndrome — a genetic disorder with both mental and physical manifestations. George had overcome many challenges to receive the highest rank Scouting offers. It took him seven years of continuous hard work, but he never gave up.

Based on his physical and mental impairments, George could have asked the BSA to waive certain requirements. George and his parents chose not to. "He wanted to earn it just like everyone else," George's mother said. "Some of the badges were very challenging for him, especially the ones that require a lot of writing and organization. It took him literally years to earn Personal Management merit badge. But he is quite a strong swimmer, and he amazes us with his direction-finding abilities."

George's Eagle project was to landscape and improve the grounds of an assisted living facility for people with disabilities. He led other Scouts in planting and numerous landscaping improvements.

After completing his project, George confronted what was for him one of the most challenging aspects of all — filling out the paperwork. It took a long time, but George eventually finished.

George stood proudly on the dais with his parents beside him, smiling broadly, as he held up his well-earned framed commendation. Scoutmaster Bergen was grinning from ear to ear. "This is what it's all about," Mr. Bergen thought to himself as he walked forward and extended his left hand to his Troop's newest Eagle Scout.

BSA's standards provide some flexibility. For example, a physically challenged Scout who cannot swim can still earn Eagle. However, in many cases, objective standards are still very important.

Leadership Yarn

You never know when a Scouting lesson will occur or when an opportunity for leadership training may arise. Scoutmaster Kramer received this letter from a newly promoted Eagle Scout as the Scout was leaving for college:

"You have been my Scoutmaster for eight years now, since I was eleven years old and you taught me a lot. You have taught me about camping and the outdoors (you know more about that stuff than anyone else I have ever met), but the most important things you taught me were applicable outside of Scouting."

"You taught me about hard work and responsibility. When I was working on Emergency Preparedness Merit Badge and did a really poor job on the missing person drill, you would not accept it. You said we were disorganized and took too long to find the victim. You would not organize another one either; you made me do it. It was almost a year later before I got it done because I had to organize a campout and get kids to go just for that. At the time I thought you were a real jerk, but I see now that I got a lot more out of the experience doing it the right way and without you doing it for us."

Doing one's best is a personal and individual matter. We all fall short at times. In Scouting, we have objective standards but we also need to consider special circumstances. Doing your best is most important when it comes to living up to Scout values. In the following section, we consider ethical leadership and the shared code of conduct that we all live by as our Scout Oath, Law, Motto and Slogan.

Caring Leadership

Leadership Yarn ∽∽

It was the first day of summer camp, and newly elected Senior Patrol Leader Doug Anderson was charged up. He announced to the rest of the Patrol Leaders Council that this was going to be the best summer camp ever. "My campsite is going to run like clockwork," Doug said. "I'm going to win the Honor Camp award for this Troop!"

Brian, one of the Patrol Leaders sitting around the table, earnestly began reminding everyone about the camp's inspection procedures and how each Patrol needed to work hard to prepare for the first day's inspection — which experience had shown was often the most difficult. Senior Patrol Leader Doug cut Brian off in mid-sentence.

"We know all that already," Doug said, throwing up his hands. Doug had waited for years for his chance to shine. He was not about to let Brian or anyone else upstage him. "The important thing is we can't get a bad inspection score. I am not about to let you guys make me look bad. I'm going to get the best inspection score ever for this Troop," Doug said with determination and authority.

Finding his comments met by silence, Doug proceeded to issue orders. He was not interested in what anyone else had to say. He had it all figured out and knew exactly what he wanted to do. This summer camp was going to be the crowning achievement of his Scouting career. He was going to make sure he got all the glory he so richly deserved. Meanwhile, Doug's Patrol Leaders began thinking about all the other places in camp they'd rather be.

Many Scouts also play team sports. Teenagers learn important lessons in teamwork on the playing field, basketball court or hockey rink. They learn, for example, that even a star player usually cannot win games single-handedly. They also learn the importance of following their coach's directions. They learn when it is appropriate to show self-initiative and when one must play an assigned role. They learn the importance and logic of playing by the rules. With watchful referees penalizing nearly every violation, the players learn that most bad behavior does not win games but instead actually hurts the team rather than helping.

Scoutmasters know there are major differences between a sports team and a Scout Troop. For example, in Scouting, everyone can be a winner and nobody sits on the bench. And in Scouting, everyone is supposed to be a referee. All youth and adult members are expected to live by the shared code of conduct of the Scout Oath, Law, Motto and Slogan. In Scouting, this is not simply a collection of hopeful aspirations — it is a practical set of rules for playing our "game with a purpose." As has so often been observed, the Scout Law is not a list of "don't dos." Instead, it is a statement of fact describing what a Scout is.

Historical Perspective

As in modern times, the early part of the 20th century was a difficult time for the world's youth. Communities were trying to figure out how to reduce youth gangs, loitering, delinquency and other bad citizenship. Baden-Powell noted these conditions, and wanted his new "peace Scouts" to live by and aspire to a code of morals and ethics. He therefore included Scouting Values in his *Scouting for Boys* — the Scout Oath, Law, Motto and Slogan.

Just like the Scout Oath American Scouts now recite at every meeting, B-P's Scout Oath had three points: (1) duty to God and Country; (2) do your best to help other people at all times; and (3) obey the Scout law. Initially, B-P's Scout Law had nine points: Trustworthy, Loyal, Helpful, Friendly, Courteous, Kind, Obedient, Cheerful and Thrifty. The BSA added three more points — Brave, Clean and Reverent. B-P based the Scout Motto (Be Prepared) on his own initials. B-P also instructed Scouts to tie a square knot in their neckerchief every night to remind themselves to do a good turn the next day.

Baden-Powell was witness to the horrors of war and destruction, as well as to the privilege and power of Imperial England's upper classes. He was a good man of high moral conscience. However, unlike so many other so-called "do-gooders," B-P was not a self-righteous dreamer. He was a man of action who knew how to lead troops and accomplish missions. B-P's mission for the new Scouting program was to practice moral, ethical leadership and unselfish citizenship for England and the world. He wanted to give boys as much responsibility as possible — but always in the context of living by a set of Scouting Values dedicated to serving humanity.

Baden-Powell said:

"If I were asked what is the prevailing vice in the world I should say — Selfishness. The average man will gladly give a contribution to feed the poor and will feel satisfied that he has then done his duty, but he is not going to dock himself of his own food and good wine to effect a saving for that purpose. Selfishness exists in a thousand different ways ... To eradicate selfishness [a Scoutmaster should establish and reinforce] the Good Turn Habit. The Scouting practices tend in a practical way to educate the boy out of the groove of selfishness. Once he becomes charitable he is well on the way to overcome or to eradicate the danger of this habit."

For many of us, Baden-Powell's Scouting Values are the most important part of Scouting. Scouting Values define what it means to be a Scout. The Oath, Law, Motto and Slogan are our moral compass — they point the direction for us to follow and tell us to do the right thing.

They tell us to help other people at all times by unselfishly doing good turns and giving service to others. They also tell us to be helpful, friendly and kind to our fellow man. They direct us to be reverent to God and loyal to our country. They tell us to act with honor under all circumstances. We live our adult lives according to these Scouting Values.

If the goal of leadership is to accomplish what is best for the group, there is compelling logic to adhering to a shared code of conduct.

Have you ever magnetized iron? Before magnetizing the iron, the molecules are arranged haphazardly. But if you place the iron in a powerful magnetic field, the magnetic field aligns the molecules in a common orientation. When you take the iron out of the magnetic field, the molecules stay aligned. Because the molecules are now aligned, their individual magnetic fields add up and work together to generate a magnetic pull that can move other objects.

People can be pulled into a common orientation by human magnetism ("charisma"). People can also be pulled into a common orientation by a common set of beliefs. Leaders can use their influence to inspire the common set of beliefs.

Leadership Yarn 𝓪𝓪𝓪

It was a warm Sunday morning in June at St. Paul's Episcopal Church in the heart of Richmond Virginia. The year was 1865. The 25-year-old downtown building had miraculously survived the recent widespread destruction of the city. The pastor was at the altar, reciting centuries-old phrases from the Book of Common Prayer calling parishioners to the Lord's Supper.

Suddenly, a tall, well-dressed black man sitting in the western gallery reserved for black parishioners stood and began walking toward the communion rail. A jolt ran through the silent congregation. This black man had violated the ritual practiced every Sunday throughout the South for as long as anyone could remember — Whites always received communion before Blacks.

Those who had been preparing to stand and advance to the communion rail froze. The parishioners retained their kneeling positions in solemn silence and did not move. The pastor, standing before the congregation, was embarrassed and at a loss to know what to do. The black man was now kneeling at the rail to receive communion.

After a few heartbeats that seemed like an eternity, a man in his late fifties stood up from his customary pew and began walking forward toward the communion rail. The man was tall and impeccably dressed. He walked up the aisle with determination and authority. The grey of his hair, beard and moustache along with the furrows of his brow showed premature age. The last few years had been hard.

With quiet dignity, former Confederate Commanding General Robert E. Lee knelt at the rail not far from the black man and with him, awaited communion. The proud people of Richmond followed.

Ethics and Caring in Developing Servant Leadership

Some might argue that no Scoutmaster can successfully make an ethical, caring person out of an unethical, uncaring one. Parents often instill values in their children at a very young age. On the other hand, few Scoutmasters think of their roles simply as leaders of boys clubs. We would like to think that we are fostering good ethics and caring citizenship. Anecdotal stories abound about how young men at ethical crossroads have made more ethical decisions because of the example and encouragement of their Scoutmasters.

One of B-P's objectives was to substitute service to others in place of selfishness. Caring about others is an essential ingredient in effective leadership. Leaders who care about their followers are more effective than leaders who do not.

The "secret" many leadership schools teach is how effective leaders need to care about each individual in the group. Leading the group means leading each individual in the group. A leader must earn the loyalty of his followers. Loyalty must flow from the top down as well as from the bottom up. A leader has a right to expect loyalty from subordinates, but only if the leader is loyal to his subordinates.

Team members want to make a difference and be recognized for it. Leaders need to know the qualities and characteristics of each member of the team if they are to make effective use of the resources available to them. Team leaders who take a personal interest in each member of the team are more effective than those who do not.

A leader who acts primarily out of self-interest will not be respected or followed for very long — especially in Scouting or other volunteer environments. The saying "There is no 'I' in 'TEAM'" applies especially to leaders. If it is all about you, then it is not about the team. "All for one" must go in lockstep with "one for all."

Ethics from the Top Down: Setting the Example

Unselfish Scouting Values are not just for kids — they apply to anyone who wears the uniform. Baden-Powell was not heavy-handed about it, but it is clear that he intended Scouting Values to have a beneficial effect on adult leaders as well as on boys. Good Scoutmasters we have talked to agree that Scouting Values have changed their lives as adults. Adherence to a shared moral code has made us all better people.

Baden-Powell said:

"As you come to teach these things you will very soon find (unless you are a ready-made angel) that you have to acquire them yourself before you can succeed with the boys, and when once this is accomplished the occupation is intensely interesting and improving."

None of us are "ready-made angels" — we all have work to do. Scoutmasters "teach" ethics and sensitivity to others mostly by example. Our Scouts will individually and collectively think about many of the things we do — especially those things we do when we think no Scout is watching. Having our actions take on so much significance is a powerful motivator to "do the right thing." This is not because we are "do-gooders" but because setting the example is logical, consistent and the key to effective leadership and maintaining proper discipline.

Any parent of teenagers will tell you "it's not what I say, it's what I do." Give all the speeches you want, but if your children catch you doing something you told them they shouldn't do, you have wasted your breath and damaged your credibility. The word "integrity" has come to mean "of high moral standing" but the word derives from the same word as "integer" meaning "whole" or "one single entity." Well-intentioned hypocrites have no integrity at all.

Leadership Yarn

Scoutmaster Thompson was concerned. It was not the Scouts that worried him. It was the adults — one in particular. Doug Drake wore the silver epaulettes and shoulder patch of a newly-minted Assistant District Commissioner, but had rearranged his busy schedule, clearing the weekend to spend with his son and the Troop out here in the woods

Scoutmaster Thompson ambled over to Mr. Drake's empty tent and peered inside. What he saw disappointed him: a twelve-pack of beer and some fireworks. This was no time to beat around the bush. Thompson pulled Drake aside.

"Doug," he said, "you have some things in your tent you need to lock in the trunk of your car. We don't allow those things on our Troop campouts."

"Don't worry," Mr. Drake said, "the boys will never see those things. I brought them for the adults. They stay in my tent until after the last boy has gone to bed," he said with a wink.

"Look Doug, we all like to have fun, but there's a time and place for everything. As Scoutmaster, I cannot allow those things to be here. If a Scout got into them, there would be no way to explain it to his parents. You and I are wearing The Uniform. We need to set the example. You need to lock that stuff in your trunk."

Drake knew Thompson was right. "Thompson, you take life way too seriously. But I'll do as you say. You're the Scoutmaster."

If leaders are always honest, those that follow them will do their best to be honest too. If Leaders show enthusiasm and cheerfulness, those they lead will be enthusiastic and cheerful. If leaders act with conviction that "every job worth doing is worth doing right," the younger Scouts will try to do their best. If leaders demonstrate success, their followers working together will be successful. If Leaders show reverence and patriotism, those that follow will be inclined to do likewise. If leaders treat others with respect, they will inspire others to be respectful.

Instilling Strong Values

Beyond being a good role model who sets a good example, some additional techniques can be effective in getting Scouts to think about ethics in their daily lives. Here are some ideas we use in our Troop:

Scout Oath and Law: We start each meeting with the Scouts reciting the Scout Oath and Law and we make sure all adult Scouters recite them too.

Youth Protection: We are serious about our Scouts' safety and observe two-deep adult leadership at all times.

Good Turns and Service to Others: We make sure the Troop plans and participates in service projects and good turns. We make a big deal out of these opportunities and instill pride in the results.

Scoutmaster Minutes: We try to conclude every Troop meeting and Patrol Leaders Council meeting with a short, meaningful, effective Scoutmaster's Minute. It is our chance to talk directly to the Scouts about ethical decision-making.

Youth Role Models: We encourage older Scouts to stay active and engaged in the Troop and be good role models. The younger Scouts may not always be able to relate well to adults, but they will admire and emulate the older Scouts — especially those who hold leadership positions.

Discipline: We establish high standards of behavior and expect the Scouts to live up to them. We express disappointment when they do not, and take appropriate prompt action if discipline falls below minimum standards.

High Advancement Standards: Keeping advancement standards intact is important. Letting a Scout "slide" or doing him a "favor" will not benefit the Scout and will likely earn only disrespect. We make ethics a part of every Scoutmaster Conference for rank advancement. Our National Boards of Review hit it very hard with our Eagle candidates.

Scouter Presence: We try to be available to our Scouts. We believe it is important to talk to them and establish trusting interactions with them. We are always on the lookout for opportunities to counsel and mentor them. We talk to them as peers, not subordinates. We don't tolerate bullying or hazing.

Positive Attitude: We are careful about what we say about individual Scouts. Young ears are everywhere. A Scoutmaster is like a celebrity — he is always "on." Negativism and gossip have no place in our Troop.

Teaching Opportunities: We Scoutmasters are presented with countless problems during the normal operation of a troop. Whenever possible, we try to convert problems into teaching opportunities. Instead of casting blame, we turn setbacks into opportunities.

In the course of working through these kinds of issues with other adult leaders, and, if appropriate, the Patrol Leaders Council, you are teaching values and wisdom to your Scouts. Do not shy away from these "hard" issues. Confront them directly. Whenever possible and appropriate, work through the Scouts themselves (the responsible Patrol Leader for example) to resolve the situation.

The Patrol Method Misapplied

Effective but immoral leadership is exceedingly dangerous. There are many examples throughout history of evil men exercising leadership over their nations with an iron fist, but with the object of gaining and keeping power by committing crimes against humanity.

Some of these evil men have intentionally used aspects of B-P's Patrol Method to further their evil ends. For cold systematic scheming, nothing can compare to Nazi Germany's Hitler Youth ("Hitler Jugend" or "HJ"). Some have said that in the twilight of his life, even B-P himself was demoralized by how he and the international Scouting organization had been fooled. Unfortunately, B-P did not live long enough to see the great 1945 victories of democracy over fascist dictatorships.

Baldur Von Schirach testified at his Nuremburg war crimes trial that his Hitler Youth was very much like B-P's Boy Scouts, merely because the HJ participated in many activities Boy Scouts would find familiar — such as hiking and camping in the countryside.

Von Schirach's argument that the HJ was similar to B-P's Boy Scouts was preposterous. It was like saying a missile and a New England church steeple are essentially the same thing because they each reach skyward, get progressively skinnier with height and are pointed at the top.

The HJ was clearly different from the Boy Scouts because of its:

- cruel, relentless hazing

- constant anti-Semitic propaganda

- physical and mental brutality

- arrogance

- paramilitary exercises.

These differences were so profound and pervasive that on June 22, 1933, under the authority of Adolph Hitler, Von Schirach outlawed the preexisting German (BP) Boy Scouts.

Even more important, the HJ had nothing like the Scout Oath or Law that B-P made the cornerstone of Boy Scouting. Instead of the Scout Oath or Law that we know so well, Von Schirach required his HJ members to swear a terrible blood oath of unquestioning, absolute allegiance to Adolph Hitler:

> *"In the presence of this blood banner, which represents our Fuhrer,*
> *I swear to devote all my energies and my strength to the savior of*
> *our country, Adolph Hitler. I am willing and ready to give up my*
> *life for him, so help me God."*

We can all be thankful that Von Schirach's ignominious HJ came to an end when Allied forces defeated Nazi Germany in 1945. But today, some in the world are again using Von Schirach's evil formula of personality cultism, unquestioned obedience and a culture of hatred to indoctrinate young men and women to become radical terrorists.

Today's youth will become tomorrow's leaders and eventually rule the world. The legislators, judges, and executives who will lead our country 30 or 40 years from now are currently young men aged 11 through 18. Some are in your Scout Troop. There is no more important mission than to train our future leaders to be effective, ethical, caring, and to live by the Scout Oath and Law.

Training Leaders to Care about the Entire Group

The United States Marine Corps has a philosophy: "We take care of our own." The BSA's modern "servant leadership" training philosophy is perfectly consistent with this philosophy. Good leaders must genuinely care about those whom they lead. This is a tall order for the self-absorbed modern American teenager.

Leadership Yarn

The Patrol Leaders Council was meeting to plan next year's calendar. Tom, the new SPL, was leading the discussion. Owen, a 16-year-old Patrol Leader, was in favor of a backpacking trip for older Scouts only.

"No one under First Class rank should attend," Owen proclaimed.

"Have you discussed that with the other members of your Patrol?" Tom asked. Tom was looking at the Troop Patrol roster, and could see that only one member of Owen's Patrol had attained First Class.

"No," said Owen, "but they won't care. They can go on the Camporee instead." Owen had no intention of attending the Camporee if he could go on the backpack trip.

Joe, another Patrol Leader, was insistent that the Troop should not go on any camping trips during hunting season. "It's too dangerous," Joe said. "We could get shot at out there or disrupt a hunt."

Tom asked why they could not camp in protected land where hunting was not allowed. "People break those rules all the time," Joe said. Truth be told, Joe planned to hunt with his dad and uncle every single weekend during hunting season, and he did not want Troop activities to interfere with his own personal plans.

After biting his tongue and listening for some time, Scoutmaster Bergen finally decided to speak up and remind the Patrol Leaders Council that they were planning the annual calendar for everyone in the Troop — not just for themselves. "Joe, if you can't attend a certain campout because of a conflict, you can always put your assistant in charge," Mr. Bergen said.

Bergen also guided the PLC to come up with a compromise: older Scouts could go on a backpacking-style leadership camp but also had to agree to participate in the Camporee that same month for the entire Troop. The Patrol Leaders ultimately committed to this plan.

Managing Cliques

The natural result of proper application of the Patrol Method is to develop cliques. Each Patrol is a clique with a strong identity and cohesiveness.

In a modern Scout Troop, an "older Scout" clique or "cool kids" clique can be a destructive force that works against the Patrol Method. Friendships and alliances are natural and desired results of Scouting. When setting up Patrols or other Troop organizational structures, ignoring long-established friendships can lead to problems. It sometimes takes thoughtful effort by adult leadership to prevent these same forces from breaking down leadership and preventing delivery of the promise to all Scouts in the Troop.

Leadership Yarn

Brian, the newly elected Senior Patrol Leader of Troop 1143, led a contingent of Scouts to a local museum. The tour guide asked the group to divide in half. Brian turned to the Scouts. "All the cool kids stick with me," Brian announced. "That means Ed, Hans, Luis, Joe and Johnny. All the rest of you Scouts are in the other group." The Scouts arranged themselves just as they had been told. The "cool" kids were of course bursting with pride at having been selected for the first group. The Scouts passed over to the second group felt demoralized and inferior. Some of them felt like leaving and just going home. They were not happy following their new Senior Patrol Leader after he had dissed them so publicly and without any reason.

Brian's actions did not go unnoticed. He soon found himself sitting before a Board of Review. The Troop Committee was interested in exploring with Brian how exclusion has no place in Scouting.

History teaches us glaring examples of what happens under unethical leadership. We have a responsibility to teach ethical caring leadership. But executing well requires more than good intentions. In the next section, we focus on planning and on some lessons we have learned in our Troop about teaching the average American teenager how to plan.

Planning: How to Facilitate Without Taking Over

Leadership Yarn 〰〰〰〰〰〰〰〰〰〰〰〰〰〰〰〰〰〰〰〰〰〰〰〰〰〰〰〰〰〰

Venture Crew 700 voted in December to go on a seven-day bike hike in late June. Mr. Lockhart, the adult Advisor, asked Crew Leader Justin to begin holding monthly organizational meetings beginning in January so the Crew could adequately plan the bike hike.

By February, Justin had purchased maps at the local outdoors store and had researched the route on the Internet. To Mr. Lockhart's mind, however, the Crew accomplished little during the early spring organizational meetings beyond talking about how much fun they were going to have and what kind of bikes they were going to buy or borrow.

Finally, during a meeting in early May, Advisor Lockhart showed his frustration by asking many hard questions. The Scouts had no answers. Mr. Lockhart demanded that the Scouts produce a written plan. He made it clear that he was not going to be the one to write it.

Mr. Lockhart was clear about what he expected of the written plan in terms of level of detail and scope. He also told the Crew why the written plan was essential: "Not just for those of us going on the trip, but also for safety reasons — those staying behind need to know where we will be each night."

Mr. Lockhart left the May meeting frustrated and disappointed. The Scouts, meanwhile, were scratching their heads trying to figure out what was wrong with Mr. Lockhart — after all, their trip was still over six weeks away!

Mr. Lockhart was so concerned about the Scout's lack of planning that he was ready to cancel the entire trip. To save the trip, he was tempted to sit down at his computer, write the first draft of a detailed plan himself, and email it to Justin, who could then edit it.

But Mr. Lockhart listened to his gut. His Wood Badge training informed him that this would be the wrong approach. "Never do something a Scout can do," his inner voice told him. So instead, Mr. Lockhart did some web searches to learn more about bike hike safety issues, and took a "wait and see" attitude. He resolved to cancel the trip a week beforehand if the Scouts failed to produce the written plan he had asked for.

Mr. Lockhart was right to have listened to his Wood Badge instincts. The Scouts' preparations kicked into high gear as soon as high school final exams were over. The Scouts began meeting informally to discuss and evaluate equipment and schedule. They went to camping and bike stores and purchased food and spare bike supplies. They began writing their plan down.

What Mr. Lockhart finally realized; he had been unfairly trying to impose his own adult expectations of planning and certainty onto the Scouts. The Scouts planned differently than Mr. Lockhart would have, and they planned on a different time scale — but they did plan and did not overlook anything important once they got going.

Mr. Lockhart decided to take more of a "go with the flow" attitude and began trusting the Crew Leader to plan and to lead. He set realistic but firm expectations for the type of planning he expected. He told the Scouts "The Why" of planning (to be able to leave behind a written itinerary so parents and other Crew support would know where the Crew expected to camp each night during the trip). He also reduced his stress level and stopped fretting.

The trip was a huge success and a lot of fun. The Crew Leader had left enough flexibility in the plan to allow time for spontaneous activities. The Crew stopped to pick blackberries and took a detour to see a waterfall the Scouts learned about on the trail from some hikers. These serendipitous activities ended up being among the highlights of the trip.

The BSA has recently devoted a lot of attention to planning and accomplishing goals with its NYLT Vision/Goals/Planning, SMART Goals, and Planning and Problem Solving Tool. Good planning takes lots of practice — and in our experience it is more art than science.

Remember the conversation Alice had with the Cheshire Cat?

"Would you tell me, please, which way I ought to go from here?" asked Alice.

"That depends a good deal on where you want to get to," said the Cat.

"I don't much care where," said Alice.

"Then it doesn't matter which way you go," said the Cat.

How do you help Scouts to plan without taking over the process yourself?

Let's face it. The average teenage boy has trouble planning anything beyond what he is going to eat for lunch — and even that is typically last minute catch-as-catch-can. How do you get Scouts to do the advanced planning necessary to execute something complex, like a big spring bike hike or a caving expedition?

Say the Scouts want to go on a 20-mile hike and overnight camp. Super! But where? When? Who? Got transportation? Food? Permits? Need to reserve a campsite?

How is the team going to take care of all these details? Scoutmasters are not supposed to do it all. Instead, we leave it up to the Patrol Leaders Council and the Patrols to figure it out — with our mindful eyes watching the process and with us gently mentoring without taking over.

Plan Plan Plan!

Before doing anything, leaders must come up with a plan. You cannot exercise leadership wisely without an action plan. Planning must take place at all levels. Planning is continuous.

Sometimes, a plan is something you come up with at the spur of the moment — it is more like a reaction to a specific situation. For example, our first aid training teaches us that upon seeing uncontrolled bleeding, we must move fast! Elevate the wound; apply direct pressure and then arterial pressure. In our mind, we would come up with a simple plan immediately:

1. grab a cloth (handkerchief, shirt, etc.) — preferably clean

2. fold it a couple of times

3. place the cloth on the wound and elevate it

4. apply direct pressure and, if necessary, arterial pressure

5. have someone call "911."

Putting together an event for a number of other people takes more planning. For more elaborate activities that coordinate many participants and involve teamwork, more time is needed to come up with a detailed plan. Just recall your latest Life Scout's attempt to put together the plan for his Eagle Project. How many times did you need to review and comment on what he proposed?

Scouts might ask, "Why do I need to plan? Why can't we just go out and do it?" They might think at first that spending time sitting there talking and thinking about what they are going to do is a big waste of time.

Scouts need to appreciate that careful planning will reduce errors and the need to correct errors — especially in the outdoors where it may take some time to recover.

Careful planning also helps with teamwork and confidence building. Good advanced planning is like turning on the afterburner of an F-16 Fighter. It is a way for Scouts to increase the likelihood of success despite their relative inexperience. Scout leaders feel more confident and prepared when armed with a good plan.

We have found that major conflict arises in our Troop when adults apply their own planning expectations to the Scouts. Scouts generally have not yet developed the organizational skills needed to do detailed planning. Some parents never give their sons a chance to plan anything — the parents make all the decisions and plan everything.

We sometimes find ourselves trying to get the Scouts to plan in much more detail than they ever would themselves. We try to maintain a good balance — we ask ourselves periodically what degree of planning is necessary for this particular activity. Ice climbing requires an intense amount of advanced preparation and planning, but a weekend campout to a local park probably does not. We encourage the Scouts to think through important logistical items that really have to be planned in advance to ensure a successful group event. However, we resist the temptation to impose an adult "Type A" planning expectation. Keeping a plan flexible can lead to wonderful opportunities that would otherwise be lost or perhaps not even noticed.

Leadership Yarn

Ultra-organization was one of the secrets to Tom's success at work. When Tom volunteered to be Scoutmaster of Troop 672, he began using these same techniques to organize his Scout Troop.

Tom came up with magnificent written plans for each Scouting event. Each plan was a detailed recipe with systematic instructions for how to put everything together and in what order. Tom posted these plans to the Troop website and distributed them in hard copy form to everyone well in advance of events.

Tom suggested that his plans needed to be followed to the letter. For one weekend campout, Tom told the Troop as he proudly handed them his 20-page plan: "I don't want anything to go wrong. I spent more than thirty hours putting together this plan, and I think I have thought of just about everything. If you see something you think I may have missed, let me know and I will fix it. Each Patrol Leader has lots of responsibility under this plan. I expect you to do your best to execute. If we all follow this plan, we're going to have a great time!"

Tom was right — his "Leadership By Detailed Written Instruction" yielded consistently good results. His events ran like clockwork. Every Scout knew exactly what he was supposed to do. The parents had confidence that everything was under control and their sons were being properly cared for. Everything was working out great!

At some point during his first year as Scoutmaster, Tom stumbled across some of Green Bar Bill's essays on the Internet. After some soul searching, Tom decided to try a modified approach to planning. He continued writing down detailed planning outlines for his own benefit, but he also began having his Senior Patrol Leader call more Patrol Leaders Council meetings. Instead of handing out completed written plans to dictate to the Troop how an event should go, Tom began keeping his plans to himself. He prepared outlines to help him mentor the Senior Patrol Leader and the Patrol Leaders Council to work through the logistical and organizational challenges of putting Troop events together. Tom resolved to have the patience to let the Scouts do it themselves and to not force his ideas on his Scouts.

Tom found his new approach not only worked but was highly effective. The Patrol Leaders and Senior Patrol Leader began creating and "owning" their plans. They began feeling much more important to the operation of the Troop. The Scouts didn't always do things exactly the way Tom would have suggested, but they often came up with ideas that Tom would never have thought of. Best of all, Tom was now teaching his Scouts important organizational and logistical life skills that would stay with them for their entire lives. The Scouts learned much more by developing their own plans under Tom's excellent mentoring and thoughtful methodical approach than they ever learned by simply executing plans Tom had drafted late at night staring at his computer screen. Tom also learned from his Scouts to be less compulsive about organizational details that made no real difference to anyone or were outside of everyone's control. Although it was a hard lesson, Tom finally came to know that achieving perfection is not nearly as important as letting the Scouts do it themselves.

Getting Scouts To Visualize a Plan

The BSA is teaching objective-based project management skills. We generally tell our Scouts to try to *visualize*, in advance, each and every step needed along the path to achieving their objective — that is, everything that needs to get done and the order in which those things should be done. Part of good planning is thinking about:

- *what* is to be accomplished?

- *what* activities must be undertaken?

- *who* is going to perform each activity?

- *when* should the activities be done?
  (Is there a deadline for each step?)

- *what* order should the work take?

- *what* equipment or other resources will be needed for each step?

- *how* and *where* will each step be performed?

One good test of a plan is whether there is enough detail so that a Scout who has not been involved in the planning process can implement the plan without having to ask too many questions.

From the Patrol Leaders Council's perspective, the planning process informs everyone and gets the Patrol Leaders to "buy in" to the plan. Their participation allows them to contribute to the plan and feel like they "own" the plan. This ownership is critical to getting full cooperation and enthusiasm. If the Patrol Leaders do not believe in the plan, then they will not be able to sell it to their Patrols.

The Senior Patrol Leader must lead this discussion to keep it on track and to make sure the final plan makes sense. The Patrol Leaders Council is the proper forum. A weekend leadership camp for annual program planning and leadership training can provide an opportunity to mix learning with fun and teambuilding.

Usually, putting a plan into words can help it come together. This is why the BSA requires Eagle Leadership Project plans to be in writing. By verbalizing their plans, our Scouts often get feedback and ideas they individually had not thought of that will make the plan better. This means we Scoutmasters must be good listeners and let the Scouts do most of the talking.

There are many benefits to having Scouts write down their event plans, including:

* Getting organized — make sure nothing has been missed

* Visualizing how and whether the plan is going to come together successfully

* Helping everyone remember what to do next

* Giving others confidence that the event will be worthwhile

* Communicating the plan to others and preparing them for the event

* Ensuring safety because people staying behind know where the unit is and what it is doing

* Making it easier to evaluate during and after execution

* Writing the plan can be done creatively, such as by storyboarding, to make planning more fun.

What Do You Write Down?

Some people like to write down everything — all the details. Others like to write down a few notes to remind them. Some folks like to draw pictures, some like to make lists, still others like to draw flowcharts or make checklists. There is no single right way. Different kinds of plans often need different kinds of write-ups. On page 106 is a flowchart-type plan for building a pioneering signal tower. You can use this plan to illustrate how Scouts can come up with their own plans.

In Scouting, we plan many events that are similar from one repetition to the next. With practice, planning becomes easier. As Scouts plan, they gain experience and confidence and can teach each other how to plan.

Sometimes forms are useful to help structure the planning process. A **Patrol Activity Planner** (on page 107) might help your Patrols plan activities. Make several copies of this or rewrite it on a piece of paper and have the Patrols fill in the blanks during their meetings.

How to Build a Tower

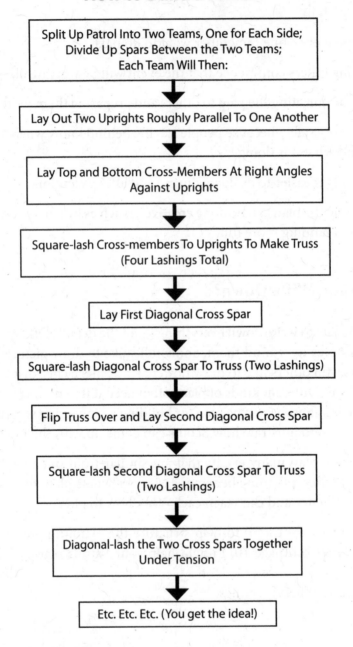

Split Up Patrol Into Two Teams, One for Each Side;
Divide Up Spars Between the Two Teams;
Each Team Will Then:

↓

Lay Out Two Uprights Roughly Parallel To One Another

↓

Lay Top and Bottom Cross-Members At Right Angles
Against Uprights

↓

Square-lash Cross-members To Uprights To Make Truss
(Four Lashings Total)

↓

Lay First Diagonal Cross Spar

↓

Square-lash Diagonal Cross Spar To Truss (Two Lashings)

↓

Flip Truss Over and Lay Second Diagonal Cross Spar

↓

Square-lash Second Diagonal Cross Spar To Truss
(Two Lashings)

↓

Diagonal-lash the Two Cross Spars Together
Under Tension

↓

Etc. Etc. Etc. (You get the idea!)

Patrol Activity Planner

Patrol Name: _____ Troop # _____

Activity: _____ Activity Date/Time: _____

Equipment needs: _____

_____

Advancement Opportunities: _____

_____

Task Assignments	Scout	When Needed
1. _____	_____	_____
2. _____	_____	_____
3. _____	_____	_____
4. _____	_____	_____
5. _____	_____	_____
6. _____	_____	_____
7. _____	_____	_____
8. _____	_____	_____
9. _____	_____	_____
10. _____	_____	_____

Troop Annual Planning

When you go out hiking, you usually know where you are going. You have a map, a compass, and a GPS. Without them, you would just wander around.

The Troop needs a map for its annual program. This is important for scheduling activities and determining what Patrol planning will entail for those events. Everyone can then see the program for at least the next three or four months and hopefully for the entire year. The plan is also a great recruiting device because it shows the Troop does not just warm their chairs attending weekly meetings.

To set the Troop's direction, the Patrol Leaders Council should figure out:

* what do they want to do?

* what will it take to do it?

* when do they want to do it?

* who will do what and by when?

The Patrol Leaders Council should do the planning. **The Troop Monthly Planner** or an ordinary calendar will help the Patrol Leaders Council plan the activities for their Troop. It ought to be completed in consultation with the Scoutmaster, for each month of Troop program.

Many activities are established by the local Scout Council and District and should be considered during the planning. Also, note all the holidays and other competing activities (like the local school sports schedule, Prom night, Homecoming, and final exam week).

Here is how our Scribe uses the Planner or a calendar:

* fill in the name of the month

* identify the month's theme

* list the dates and activities that will support the theme

* identify which Patrol will be responsible for which activities.

Put each month in a notebook to create the annual (or semi-annual or quarterly) plan. The Patrol Leaders Council should plan well in advance to be sure early registration such as for summer camp, Philmont, Seabase, or Northern Tier happens.

The plan developed at Patrol Leaders Council planning meetings might look something like this for one quarter:

January: Theme — Winter Camping

               Outing — Klondike Derby Camporee

               Skills — Winter First Aid

               Leadership Skill — Teamwork and Effective

               Use of Group Resources

               [Implementation Details]

February: Theme — Winter Sports

               Outing — Ski Trip to Seven Springs

               Skills — Group Safety

               Leadership Skill — Effective Communications

               [Implementation Details]

March: Theme — Orienteering

               Outing — Backpacking Hike Up Old Ragg Mountain

               Skills — Map, Compass, GPS, Grids

               Leadership Skill — Effective Planning

               [Implementation Details]

Continue to do this for each month in the Troop year. Some of the plan may become "institutionalized" as events the Troop participates in each year. That can ease the planning work significantly if the Patrol Leaders Council wishes to continue the same events but can also create a "tradition" that can be hard to break away from. Sometimes you need to remind your Patrol Leaders Council of its ability to take new directions instead of taking the safer, well-worn, but potentially less interesting path.

The Patrol Leaders Council needs to plan continuously throughout the year to work out the details for each Troop meeting and every other activity (campouts and other outings, Courts of Honor, service projects, etc.). Troops do it in different ways, but we have found the best time to have a monthly planning meeting is probably about the middle of the previous month so Scouts have plenty of time to make arrangements.

Resist the temptation to plan during Troop meeting time. Younger Scouts will become bored. The Patrol Leaders Council should be planning exciting meetings for those younger Scouts in advance, not forcing them to become part of the planning team.

The Patrol Leaders Council can use the **Troop Meeting Planner** on page 112 to help plan Troop meetings. Another good aid is the official BSA publication *Troop Program Planning*. It will give your Patrol Leaders Council great ideas about detailed meeting and activity plans for many different program themes.

Please also refer to the BSA's leadership training course materials on planning. Some of the approaches presented in those materials are especially helpful in getting adolescents to understand the whys and hows of planning.

In the next section, we explore ways to share leadership in a Scout Troop. Some leadership styles we explore in the next section might make you smile as you recognize leaders you have encountered in the past. You might consider how the planning techniques of this section relate to ways to share leadership described next.

Troop Monthly Planner

Month: _____ Theme: _____

Date	Activity	Responsible Patrol
_____	_____	_____
_____	_____	_____
_____	_____	_____
_____	_____	_____
_____	_____	_____
_____	_____	_____
_____	_____	_____
_____	_____	_____
_____	_____	_____
_____	_____	_____
_____	_____	_____
_____	_____	_____
_____	_____	_____
_____	_____	_____

Troop Meeting Planner

Meeting Date: _____ Theme: _____

Pre-Meeting Activity: _____ Patrol

_____ _____

Opening Ceremony: Patrol

_____ _____

Skill Lesson(s): Patrol

_____ _____

_____ _____

_____ _____

Game: Patrol

_____ _____

Scoutmaster's Minute: SM/ASM

_____ _____

Closing Ceremony: Patrol

_____ _____

Notes: _____

_____

_____

Next Meeting's Theme: _____

Scouting Is Fun!

Scouting is the adventure of backpacking up a steep trail through the woods and over rocks, following blazes to get to high places few ever reach.

Scouting is the excitement of waking up under canvas to a full day of rifle shooting, archery, swimming, canoeing, fishing and other fun camp activities.

Scouting is the fellowship of sitting around a bright campfire, telling stories and talking with your buddies as countless stars shine down from a vast velvety-black sky.

Scouting is the accomplishment of working together to start a fire on a frosty cold morning so you can cook a hot breakfast that will keep you going on the trail all day long.

Scouting is the challenge and fun of playing games that test Patrol skills and teamwork.

Scouting is good citizenship and unselfish service to others.

Scouting is God and Country — reverence to God and patriotism to our great nation.

Scouting is the fellowship of a National or International Jamboree, where thousands of Scouts from different cultures and backgrounds get together to share their enthusiasm for the greatest youth program in the world.

Scouting is the honor and solemnity of an Eagle ceremony recognizing a Scout who has achieved Scouting's highest award.

Scouting is all these things ... and more! Scouting is the lessons and memories that stay with you wherever you go and whatever you do.

Shared Leadership

Leadership Yarn

The PLC planned a cooking demonstration for the Troop's annual Brownsea campout. Older Scouts were to teach the new Scouts how to make beef stew in a Dutch oven. The entire Troop (including the adults) would eat the results for dinner. 15-year-old Troop Guide George Sanders volunteered to lead the cooking demonstration.

George had never been a patrol leader. He was not used to delegating or getting a team to work together. He had always found it easier to do it all himself. He knew it would get done right that way.

When the time came to prepare the meal, George did not ask any other older Scout to help or participate. Instead, he put wood onto the fire to make coals, and began cutting up onions and bacon. Other Scouts were sitting around the fire, but George did not ask them for help, nor did they offer. Working alone, George proceeded to assemble the beef stew in a vast 16-inch Dutch oven. By this time, he had a nice bed of coals. He lifted the Dutch oven and placed it carefully into the fire ring to heat and simmer. He put some coals on the lid and arranged them carefully for even heating.

The Senior Patrol Leader soon called George away to help organize a Capture the Flag game. George checked the stew one last time. It was simmering nicely. Satisfied that all was in order, George ran off to help with the wide area game. He left no one in charge of the group's dinner.

New Scouts returned from their advancement activities and sat around the fire ring. The fire was a huge temptation for the new Scouts, who loved stoking it and making big flames. The new Scouts began heaping on wood. The fire burned higher and higher. No one moved the Dutch oven. The new Scouts had no idea how to maintain a Dutch oven at simmering temperature. The Dutch oven containing their dinner remained in its same position, near what was now an inferno.

With the fire built up, the stew reached cremation temperature. Most of the water boiled out, and the stew began to burn. Soon the entire bottom was charred. What remained was barely edible. Instead of giving George kudos for making a great meal, the others blamed George for burning up their dinner.

George was supposed to be demonstrating dutch oven cookery to the new Scouts. He could easily have involved the new Scouts in helping him to put the ingredients together. Lots of older Scouts were also available to help. Instead of involving others, George decided to prepare dinner alone. Even though he performed this task well, consequences of his failure to involve others impacted everyone.

AUTHORITARIAN / DO-IT-ALL   DELEGATING / MENTORING   CONSENSUS / JOINING IN

SHARED LEADERSHIP SPECTRUM

Don't Be "Mr. Do-It-All"

We have all been in situations where our failure to coordinate and plan in advance forces us to do-it-all-by-ourselves. However, the yarn you just read illustrates how someone could choose to do it all by himself instead of leading. A Mr. Do-It-All is a human dynamo! His style is often one of:

- a loner – not a team player
- not asking for input from others but just doing what has to be done – as he defines it
- rarely explaining "The Why"
- often convinced he knows best
- may like the control
- may have trouble trusting others
- may want to take all the credit, even for the efforts of others
- "Mr. Indispensable"
- high or over-achiever
- often over-worked and not getting things done
- may expend super-human effort while others stand around
- often leaves others out
- may be apt to take new ideas as criticisms.

Why would a Scout leader try to do it all himself? Some leaders cannot seem to ask others for help. Some folks do not trust others enough to delegate, and think they are the only ones who can properly implement a task or direction. Some leaders feel the need to control all group activities and take credit for all group successes. A leader may be unable to delegate if he cannot tolerate less-than-perfect performance. Trouble trusting others may be an issue.

Whatever the reason, this kind of leader often ends up micromanaging every activity. Followers are constantly second-guessed and overruled. They are rarely given adequate information or authority to contribute effectively. What is wrong "leading" like "Mr. Do-It-All"?

- team players get more done and have more fun

- no one likes to stand around and just watch

- Mr. Do-It-All might be liked but probably not respected as a leader

- the group won't "own" the event if they can't help

- no one offers new ideas because Mr. Do-It-All has not asked them for ideas and probably doesn't even want to hear them

- no replacement leaders are trained.

Serving under this kind of leader can be frustrating and unrewarding. Because followers are not given adequate authority and discretion, they are set up to fail or to accomplish little. Because followers tend to feel marginalized, Mr. Do-It-All often ends up having no "followers" – just "stand-arounders." In more extreme cases, would-be followers who could have been useful resources drift off to more rewarding activities outside of the Troop.

A Better Way: Sharing Leadership by Delegating

Anyone who has ever tried to shovel snow off of a long driveway or dig a long ditch alone knows the power of teamwork. You accomplish much more working with others than working by yourself, and you have much more fun doing it.

Nobody likes to let go. Some folks tend to think they can do it better than anyone else. Maybe some can. But failing to delegate causes all kinds of problems that ultimately weaken the Troop. Instead of doing it all yourself, you'll have more fun if you share your leadership and delegate.

Even more importantly, the Patrol Method depends on shared leadership and delegation. For the Patrol Method to work, the Scoutmaster must delegate real authority to his Patrol Leaders and other boy leaders. This will inevitably lead to less-than-perfect results, but the tradeoff is worth it.

On the Troop level, the Senior Patrol Leader is ultimately responsible for maintaining and purchasing Troop equipment, keeping Troop records, organizing Troop activities and many other tasks. To get these jobs done, he appoints Assistant Senior Patrol Leaders, Guides or Instructors to have authority in different areas. The Senior Patrol Leader does not run every Troop skill training session or game himself. Instead, he asks Patrol Leaders to take charge of different tasks. Each week, a different patrol can be assigned as service patrol and ceremony patrol. Within a patrol, the Patrol Leader can use a duty roster to delegate tasks to patrol members.

By delegating authority, a leader does not need to worry about the details of how those tasks get done. All he needs to do is to make sure the person to whom he has delegated responsibility is doing his job and is not over his head. Sharing leadership by delegation makes the leader's job easier and gives other Scouts a chance to learn and contribute. Delegation is essential to the Patrol Method.

Despite its power and importance, delegating is perhaps the most difficult leadership skill to practice effectively. The following yarn illustrates what can happen when delegation fails.

Leadership Yarn

The Patrol Leaders Council was planning the Troop's annual potluck Holiday Party. When Senior Patrol Leader Ken asked for volunteers, each Patrol Leader stepped up to do his part. Max, the Patrol Leader of the Spartans, volunteered to bring snacks. Tom said his Border Patrol would bring main courses. The Singing Hobos offered to bring the drinks, and the Plan B Patrol was happy to bring desserts. The Troop Scribe dutifully noted the various assignments.

The Patrol Leaders Council was ready to move on to the next topic, but Ken knew that Webelos Cub Scouts had been invited to attend the party. He wanted to make sure the Cubs would have a fun time. So Ken suggested: "I also think we need a program for the party."

"What do you mean 'program'?" Max inquired.

"What we're going to do at the party," Ken responded.

"Maybe we can sing carols," Tom suggested. The other Patrol Leaders groaned. "Won't just eating and talking be enough?" Max wailed. "We have a flag ceremony and announcements. What's wrong with that?"

"I think each Patrol should do a skit or cheer," Ken said. The SPL knew that skits were a great way to make the party fun. He also knew skits would hold the interest of the visiting Cubs. No one objected. In fact, nobody said anything. Ken did not take a vote, nor did he explain why he thought it was important to have skits. "You can practice your skits at the next Troop meeting," he said. "We have lots of time before the party."

Ken had to miss the next Troop meeting because of a holiday band concert, and he forgot to tell his assistant to follow up on the skits. The Patrol Leaders did not follow up either. Some simply forgot. Others did not think much of the idea and did not push it with their patrols.

The big night arrived a week later. Everyone was in a festive mood. The Patrols brought lots of food. There were more snacks and desserts and fewer main courses than the adults would have arranged, but the Scouts thought the food was perfect.

Just before calling the Holiday Party to order, Senior Patrol Leader Ken pulled his Patrol Leaders aside. "Do you want to perform your skits before or after the meal?" he asked. The Patrol Leaders all gave him blank stares. "Skits?" Max asked. Tom looked down at his shoelaces, realizing he had never even talked to his Patrol about a skit. Another Patrol Leader said his Patrol had been working on a skit but it was not yet ready so he preferred not to do it. Not one Patrol was prepared to do a skit.

"So what are we going to do?" Ken asked in frustration. "There's lots of food," said Max, the Patrol Leader who originally thought food was all you needed for a good party.

"Look guys, I expected more," Ken said with disappointment. "If you didn't want to do skits, you should have said so at the PLC."

Ken thought about trying to pull something together at the last minute. Maybe the skit his old Patrol had performed at summer camp would work. But ultimately, *he decided against it. "No," he thought to himself, "I'm not going to try to save the day all by myself."*

The Scoutmaster Staff supported his decision and did not intervene. As anyone could have predicted, the party was still fun, but the Cubs were bored. They were used to lots of adult-planned activities in their Pack. Some wondered aloud whether Boy Scouts would be as much fun as Cub Scouts had been.

The Senior Patrol Leader learned some important lessons that night. He learned that when people do not do what is expected of them, it is the leader who is left holding the bag. You can delegate authority, but you cannot delegate responsibility. He also learned that it pays to listen to his Patrol Leaders and invite comments. He also needed to tell The Why. None of the Patrol Leaders were crazy about the skit idea, but they also did not understand that Ken was proposing skits to engage visiting Webelos. If Ken had encouraged a fuller discussion at the PLC meeting, the PLC could have arranged some different activity – maybe a piñata or a game.

How to Delegate

Delegation must be clear and unambiguous. A leader usually should not undercut the authority he delegates by trying to "co-lead." Doing so causes unclear direction and confusion.

Leadership Yarn

About two months before the district's First Aid Meet, Program Vice Chair Todd began working closely with his new Activities Chair Sarah to plan the event. The two met a few times after district committee meetings and roundtables to discuss logistics and divide up responsibilities. Problem was, Todd never made it clear who was actually in charge of the event. Todd assumed Sarah was going to run it and that he would be supporting her. Meanwhile, the way Todd interacted with Sarah signaled to her that Todd did not yet trust her enough to put her in charge. She therefore thought she was just supporting Todd and that Todd would chair the event.

Sarah lined up the site and made some calls to ensure Troop participation, just as she had promised. But since Todd never told Sarah she was in charge, Sarah naturally assumed that Todd was taking care of all other details not specifically assigned to her.

A few weeks before the event, Sarah accepted an important work assignment that would require her to be out of town on the weekend of the First Aid Meet. She regretted not being able to attend what she was sure would be a very fun district event, but her boss said she really needed her for this assignment and it was apparent to Sarah that she wasn't all that important to the successful execution of Todd's event. After all, Todd was in charge. Besides, Sarah had completed every discrete task she had promised Todd she would do to help put the event together.

The next day, Sarah checked in with Todd to let him know that she had completed all of her assigned tasks. "The site is all lined up," she reported to Todd. "I also called the patch company. They will make sure the patches are delivered at least a week beforehand. The portajohns are ordered. I will stop by the award shop to pick up the ribbons and trophies. Julia from Troop 72 said she will be there to handle registration and check-in."

"That's terrific," said Todd. "Now what about program?"

Sarah was a little puzzled that Todd wouldn't have planned program before now. "Well, at roundtable I talked with Sam Kellerman over at Troop 672. He's an MD and offered to help. You might want to give him a call."

"Okay," said Todd, himself puzzled why Sarah hadn't organized the program already and why she was asking him to call Doc Kellerman. "There's not much time, but I guess I could give Sam a call if you want me to. Now, do you intend to keep score or should we line up someone else to do that?"

"I'll be out of town that day," replied Sarah, "but I'm happy to give my Committee Chair a call to see if the district can use our scorekeeping spreadsheet. He has a great setup on a laptop with lots of battery power."

Silence. "Wait a minute. You're not going to be there?" Todd asked as he felt his stomach lurch.

"No," said Sarah. "I have to go on assignment that weekend. I'm really sorry to miss such a fun event! But it sounds like you have everything under control."

Todd began sweating. He had only a few weeks to organize the entire program for the First Aid Meet.

Todd could have blamed Sarah for letting him down, but Todd let himself down. He failed to clearly delegate to Sarah. If Sarah had clearly understood that she was in charge and essential to making the event successful, she would likely have turned down the out-of-town assignment. By not clearly delegating and instead trying to remain partly in charge, Todd had set himself up to fail. He was now forced to ask others to drop everything to help. Nobody likes last-minute surprises. The district First Aid Meet would come off, but like so many other volunteer events, it could have been so much better had Todd been more clear in the scope of his delegation.

Delegate Authority, Not Responsibility

A leader remains ultimately responsible when he delegates. By delegating authority, the leader relieves himself of the burden of worrying about all the details. He also gives others the incentive to carry through because they are responsible to him for their part of the outcome. More importantly, he gives others a chance to learn how to lead and accomplish.

In Scouting, an effective adult leader keeps the responsibility and authority where it is supposed to be – with the Scouts. He lets the Scouts take the full credit for what the group achieves. The trick is to delegate in a way that sets your followers up to succeed. The following yarn is about the ultimate form of delegation – passing the torch. It illustrates how successful delegation depends on trust and confidence.

Leadership Yarn

It was a time of war. The Scoutmaster had received his orders, and needed to leave the Troop to serve his country. He turned over the Scoutmastership to a young Assistant Scoutmaster who had recently achieved Eagle. "John," the Scoutmaster said to his Assistant, "I know you are proud of the Eagle Knot and all those other awards on your uniform. However, as Scoutmaster, they do not amount to a hill of beans. Your job now is to guide all these Scouts so they succeed. Your success will be measured not by your personal achievement, but instead by the collective achievement of your Troop. I have full confidence in you and your abilities. You have proven you are a tireless and dedicated Scout. Now you must show the same dedication to your Scouts that you showed for your own personal achievements."

Covering up or Fixing Problems Frustrates Delegation

It's true that a leader cannot delegate responsibility. However, the leader must continue to hold people responsible for what is expected of them. "Mr. Fix-It" tries to fix a problem by stepping in and doing whatever needs to be done to fix the problem. He does not make things work better. He simply covers up problems in hope that they will go away.

For example, a Senior Patrol Leader who is a "Mr. Fix-It" will complete a Patrol Leader's task instead of telling him what he did wrong and getting him to do it correctly. The Patrol Leader never learns how to improve, and hiding the problem weakens self-reliance and responsibility.

"Mr. Fix-It's" desire is order – making sure everything appears to be operating as it should even when it is not. By covering up for others, "Mr. Fix-It" relieves them of authority and self-reliance. They soon get the message that they do not need to do their best or even try very hard. After all, "Mr. Fix-It" will come along and do their job for them to make everything wonderful. Their efforts don't really matter.

Leadership Yarn

Recall the yarn at the beginning of this section about George and the burned stew? Well, here is the rest of the story:

While the Scouts were out playing Capture the Flag, Assistant Scoutmaster Fitzpatrick came along and noticed the Dutch oven close to the flames with no one minding it. "Whatever is in there isn't going to last very long under that heat!" he thought.

He found some mitts and pulled the Dutch oven off the fire. As he pulled off the lid, he could hear the crackling of stew burning on the bottom. Hardly any steam escaped. He soon discovered that all the water had boiled out. Exploratory probing with a spoon confirmed that big chunks of meat and vegetables on the bottom were blackened and burned.

The stew hissed as Fitzpatrick added water. Fitzpatrick then began trying to salvage the stew by picking out burned pieces. He found some leftover vegetables and some barley, and added them to bulk up the remainder. He then replaced the cover and put the Dutch oven back on the fire, but well off to the side where it would simmer without burning.

"Gosh, no one is going to want to eat that," thought Fitzpatrick. "I think we have another Dutch oven. Maybe I can whip something up quick with extra ingredients."

Truth be told, Fitzpatrick was a whiz at campfire cooking. Soon he had made, in a smaller Dutch oven with some leftover ingredients and a few odds and ends, some of the best chili con carne anyone ever ate on a camping trip. Trouble was, there was not enough chili to go around. "Well," he thought considerately, "since it's their first boy Scout camping trip, we'll let the new Scouts eat first."

Soon it was time to serve dinner. The Chaplain's Aide said grace, and the Scouts formed a serving line. As soon as the younger Scouts tasted the burned beef stew, they practically fought each other to get to the chili. The chili quickly disappeared. The new Scouts who had piled wood on the fire to burn their own dinner were now enjoying double helpings of restaurant-quality chili while the rest of the boys and all the adults were stuck eating the stew the new Scouts had burned up.

When asked about it later, Fitzpatrick conceded that he had made two mistakes: "My first mistake was to take any action with the burned stew beyond pulling it off the fire. I should have called the Scout down from Capture the Flag and let him deal with the consequences of his failure to delegate."

"My bigger mistake wasn't making the chili – it was my decision to serve it to the Tenderfeet! At the time, I was convinced I was acting as a caring leader. Instead, I should have reserved that chili for the adults and a few senior Scouts. The same Scouts who burned up the stew by piling wood on the fire were the ones who got to eat the chili. I took away from the new Scouts a gift: the opportunity to learn the consequences of their actions of piling wood on top of their own dinner and sitting there by the fire without paying attention or offering to help."

George and his Assistant Scoutmaster each learned valuable leadership lessons that day. George learned that it does not pay to be "Mr. Do It All." ASM Fitzpatrick learned not to be "Mr. Fix-It" and that an adult leader needs to think through what he is doing very carefully before trying to "fix" a problem caused by a Scout's failure to exercise leadership.

Following Through

In trying to juggle busy careers with Scouting activities, we all sometimes find ourselves "starting fires" we cannot fully follow through on. However, some leaders lead by starting fires, not literally, but by throwing out great ideas that create excitement, and then not following through. This type of leader might get everyone all excited about going on a hike, call a meeting to plan it, and then not follow through or even show up on the day of the event. That leaves everyone else to decide whether they will go without him. You can readily recognize this kind of leader by his traits:

- often flamboyant and animated personality

- the center of the discussion or meeting

- rarely completes anything but starts everything

- "I've got a GREAT idea!"

- confusing in his directions to his followers

- gets people all excited and then leaves them holding the bag, ill prepared to proceed, and feeling exposed and taken advantage of

- seldom shows appreciation of others' initiatives or ideas

- refuses to take responsibility

- points the finger of blame at others

- it is all about him.

People who have been burned once or twice by "The Fire Starter" learn to distrust him and his motives. They resent being abandoned in awkward, exposed positions. They often resolve to have as little as possible to do with "The Fire Starter" despite his good ideas (which may actually be very good). "Fire starters" can cause serious problems in a shared leadership context:

Leadership Yarn

Everyone was asking the same question: "Where are the Lewises?" The Scouts were all looking forward to the Native American theme program that one of the fathers, Mr. Lewis, had enthusiastically proposed for the April campout. Mr. Lewis had gotten everyone excited about the great activities they would do: tracking, wide area games, utensil-less cooking, archery and a great campfire. Mr. Lewis had offered to organize everything and bring all the materials and supplies. The Patrol Leaders Council assumed Mr. Lewis would do as he said he would, and therefore did not bother planning any additional program.

Now it was time to depart and Mr. Lewis and his son Daniel were nowhere to be seen. A call confirmed what everyone was afraid of; the Lewises were not coming after all. Daniel Lewis had a swim meet that day, and Mr. Lewis had been called out of town on business. It was up to those going to pull something together at the last minute. It would require super-human effort and still would never be as good as what could have been accomplished with pre-planning had the PLC not counted on Mr. Lewis.

Nobody intends to become the "Mr. Lewis" in the yarn you just read, but it's not uncommon for a volunteer to be unable to fully deliver on what he offered or promised. It is the responsibility of the leader or group delegating authority to make sure the person accepting the assignment has the ability to complete the assignment. Be careful not to set up your followers to fail. Try to make sure they can actually do the tasks you delegate. Check in with them periodically. You may be able to help with advice and encouragement or by giving them interim deadlines cutting up the task into bite-sized chunks. Once you have delegated authority, try not to take it back unless you absolutely must for the good of the group. Even then, consider making adjustments in a way that allows the person being relieved to save face while still understanding that more was reasonably expected.

The Big Boss – the Opposite of Shared Leadership

In an emergency, a good leader will direct what he wants others to do by issuing commands such as "Call 911!" and "Go find the Troop First Aid Kit – NOW!"

You have probably seen this command style of leadership in war movies, where the commanding officer orders his men to "take that hill!" If you have served in the military, you have likely been on both sides of this leadership style.

Scouting is supposed to be fun. Nobody likes being ordered about. In Scouting, we stay away from the authoritarian "command" style except when it is necessary. But some "leaders" are just bosses all the time. They think the only way to get things done is "It's my way or the highway." You can spot a "Big Boss" every time by his:

- often constant reminders to everyone that he's in charge

- loud voice and barking orders

- sometimes puts others in the group down and belittles them

- refuses to let most others participate in leadership

- believes the only really good ideas are the ones he came up with himself

- may have an unforgiving attitude toward errors and less-than-perfect results even when followers are doing their best

- "My way or the highway!"

- use of negative rather than positive motivation.

What is wrong with being so authoritative all the time?

- this style doesn't cultivate new ideas

- while "The Big Boss" may think he commands respect, others don't actually respect him

- nobody "buys in" to his leadership

- people follow only because they are intimidated, not because they want to.

Leadership Yarn

Assistant Scoutmaster Rogers was conducting a merit badge class in his provisional troop. He was doing all the talking, demonstrating to the Scouts his vast knowledge of first aid. He looked up and noticed for the first time that Joe, one of the older Scouts, had ear buds– not in his ears, but around his neck.

"This boy is disrespecting me!" Rogers thought to himself. "The rule is no electronics on campouts. I'll make an example out of this Scout," he decided.

Rogers put his book down and said to Joe, in front of the entire group: "You there! I'm disappointed in you. My rule is no electronics on Scouting events. Take those ear buds off immediately and put that player away in your tent."

Joe responded: "Mr. Rogers, I'm listening to you, not my tunes. My music player is off." Joe had in fact been listening intently to Rogers and taking careful notes on what Rogers had been saying.

Rogers became furious when Joe failed to comply with a direct order. What lack of respect! He wasn't about to take this insubordination from a mere Scout. "Now you listen and listen good!" Rogers barked, using the voice of authority he had heard so many use during his years in the Navy. "No electronics on Scouting events. Put that music player in your tent right now!"

What Rogers did not know and did not bother to find out: Joe had mowed lawns for two months to earn enough to buy that music player. He could not put his music player in a tent where it might go missing, and he could not accuse his fellow Scouts of being likely to steal his music player out of his tent. Joe also resented being treated like a first-grader in front of his friends, and thought Mr. Rogers was being arbitrary. So Joe just sat there and stared steely-eyed at Mr. Rogers. Joe hadn't yet figured out that he could not win a confrontation with Assistant Scoutmaster Rogers. He was about to find out.

Seconds passed. All the other Scouts looked at Rogers. Rogers knew his authority was now on the line. He had painted himself into a corner by having this conversation in front of the group. He could not back down now. "Look, young man!" Rogers barked. "You have exactly two choices. Either put that music player in your tent, or get out of this class."

"Yes, sir" said Joe, who at that moment wanted absolutely nothing to do with Rogers. Joe stood up, walked to the other side of the campsite, sat down in a chair, pulled out his First Aid Merit Badge pamphlet and began reading. He was still wearing the ear buds around his neck.

Rogers wisely decided not to follow Joe, but he could not resist trashing him in front of the others. "That, Gentlemen, is a prime example of un-Scout-like behavior. A Scout is obedient. I know the rest of you would never act like him. Now, let's get back to the merit badge."

All the other Scouts looked at Joe sitting there by himself, across the campsite. They did not know what to think. They all liked Joe. He was a star basketball player at school, and he knew his stuff. Joe had not been listening to music. Why was Mr. Rogers being such a jerk? A few thought Mr. Rogers did the right thing, and would emulate him the next time a younger Scout did not do exactly what he was told. Others thought: "the less I have to do with Mr. Rogers, the better."

Rogers made two mistakes that day. The first mistake was to assume incorrectly that Joe was disrespecting him. The second and more important mistake was having a showdown in front of the group. There were many other ways Rogers could have handled the situation. He could have joked about Joe needing a soundtrack for the merit badge class. Or he could have pulled Joe aside at a break and asked him to put the music player in his pocket. Or if bringing the music player violated a rule, he could have told Joe that he would be happy to hold the music player until the end of the event. Having a public showdown meant someone had to win and the other had to lose. Rogers couldn't afford to lose, but he ended up losing anyway by forcing a popular Scout to lose.

Unlike what you might expect, this overbearing leadership style is sometimes based on lack of self-confidence and the leader's need to convince everyone (including himself) that he is a worthwhile person. Other times, the leader has become used to a strict chain of command such as is found in the military services where orders are routinely issued and obeyed without question. But rarely is this authoritative leadership style appropriate in a Scout troop or other volunteer organization. Because the authoritarian style is based on fear and intimidation instead of positive reinforcement, it demands the Scout to "Do [what I say is] your Best – or else!"

Pick up your *Scout Handbook*. Now locate the official "Boy Scout Demerit System." Of course, you will not find it. There is no such thing. Scouting is based on positive reinforcement, not negative punishment or hazing. When moral or ethical issues are implicated, you may have no choice but to go negative. However, teenagers rarely respond well to negative reinforcement. We have found that a more encouraging, mentoring approach is usually far more effective.

Coaching and Mentoring

To support the Patrol Method and share leadership with his Patrol Leaders, a Scoutmaster gets to be a coach or mentor. Instead of giving commands or even showing how to do something, the leader gives advice. This can be very effective in empowering his followers to execute. It also usually requires the leader to know his stuff. Often, you cannot give good advice unless you know how to do it yourself.

Leadership Yarn

Bill and Johnny were assigned fire duty. They needed to get the fire going so their Patrol could cook dinner. Unfortunately, it had rained all day and there was no dry wood to be found. They tried lighting the wet wood but were getting nowhere. As the pungent fragrance of damp half-burnt tinder drifted over the campsite, Larry, the Patrol Leader, walked over to the fire ring and asked Bill and Johnny how they were doing.

"We can't get the fire going, Larry – the wood's too wet," said Bill.

Johnny nodded, "Yeah, I guess we're going to have to eat dinner cold. What do raw potatoes taste like, anyway?"

Larry, who did not like raw potatoes at all, thought a minute, and made a suggestion. "You know," said Larry, "the last time I wanted to start a fire in the rain, I split a log to get dry kindling."

"What do you mean?" asked Bill.

"Well," said Larry, "the wood in the middle of a big log stays dry no matter how wet the outside gets. If you split the log with an ax, you can get dry wood from inside the log. Also, I think I saw a downed white birch along the trail coming in. White birch bark has lots of oil in it; it will burn like crazy even when it's wet."

Bill turned to Johnny and said, "I'll go find the ax, why don't you see if you can find some of that birch bark?" They both ran off, excited to try out their new knowledge.

In this fire-starting scenario, Larry gave direction by offering good advice. He did not order Bill and Johnny to split wood nor did he do it himself. Instead, he used a much gentler, helpful and respectful technique; he made a suggestion.

Bill and Johnny will get the satisfaction of starting a fire under wet conditions, and they will learn new techniques that could help them someday in a survival situation. Best of all, the Patrol will not have to eat raw potatoes for dinner.

What if Larry had not known how to start a fire in the rain? Larry could still have made some suggestions of what to try. Larry could have gone to another resource – maybe looking in the Scout Handbook or asking another Patrol Leader – to find out what to do.

Shifting Gears – Situational Leadership

A Scoutmaster will adjust his leadership style depending on the circumstances. This is called "situational leadership." Current BSA training refers to this as "Leading EDGE™" (Explaining, Demonstrating, Guiding, Enabling). We think of it as selecting different gears on a multi-speed bike.

The idea is to shift gears depending on group dynamics and the goal. For example, a Scoutmaster will quickly learn that different Scouts require different mentoring approaches. Some Patrol leaders need more pushing, prodding and conversation. You may need to use first gear (the one for steep hills) when you interact with those Scouts. Other Patrol Leaders seem to know exactly what they want to accomplish and will rebel against undue intervention. A higher gear (for going down hills) or even coasting may work fine when interacting with them. When a Patrol Leader confronts a new situation that bewilders him, you may need to temporarily downshift to a lower gear with your mentoring/coaching style.

On the Scout level, the Patrol Leader of a newly formed or very young patrol will need to be more directive and explanative with a lot of show-and-tell. If a patrol is experienced in certain tasks, the Patrol Leader may take a more hands-off approach and do more guiding, mentoring and enabling. In the event of an emergency or other new situation, the leader will need to adjust his leadership style to become more directive.

Being a Good Follower

If somebody else is taking the lead, a good leader becomes a good follower. When a leader delegates leadership over a well-defined area of responsibility, it is his job to follow.

Leadership Yarn

Senior Patrol Leader Evan had a scheduling conflict. He could not get to the Troop's March Wilderness Campout until Saturday afternoon. He delegated leadership of the camp to Turner, his Assistant Senior Patrol Leader.

Turner had been a little nervous when the Troop went out Friday night, but by late Saturday afternoon he was doing pretty well. The camp was busy. Every Patrol was concentrating on its assigned tasks. Then, the outdoor serenity was shattered by a loud car horn blowing. Evan's car was coming down the lane to camp. He was blasting his horn to announce his arrival.

Evan jumped out of the car and shouted "Turner! How are we doing? I'm ready to take over now!"

Turner was crestfallen. He finally had his shot at leading the Troop on a major outing and he really did not need "Mr. Important" trying to save the day before it was even in jeopardy. Nevertheless, he made his report to Evan: "I have all the Patrol Leaders organizing their people to gather building materials for shelters and bedding. Some are building cooking racks and designing techniques for no-utensil cooking. Others are laying in a good supply of wood for the night fires that will keep the shelters warm. I have assigned the Raccoon Patrol to be in charge of the campfire program, and the Cheetahs are going to build the campfire. Everything is on schedule and under control."

"Good job, Turner. I'll just call a quick Patrol Leaders Council meeting and get a report from all the Patrol Leaders to make sure they're doing what they're supposed to."

"Evan, I don't think we have time for that," an irritated Turner responded, his face flushing red. "It'll be dark soon and the guys have to get their shelters done before dinner."

Evan started to comment when an Assistant Scoutmaster stepped in to intervene. The ASM had been silently listening to the entire conversation. He quickly pulled Evan aside, walked a few feet away so they were out of Turner's hearing, and mentored Evan on the benefits of leaders sometimes being good followers. He encouraged Evan to let Turner get on with being the leader of this camp.

Evan listened and took the advice. Turner did just fine. The rest of the weekend, Evan tried not to take over – although everyone could tell it was a painful case of "follower-itis." Instead, Evan let Turner shine and made himself available to Turner as a resource. Evan realized that it was to his credit as a good leader to be a good follower and a good delegator.

Being a good follower can be harder than being a good leader. When we teach "good following" to our Scouts, we emphasize the following:

+ be unselfish

+ be patient

+ support the leader

+ understand that there is more than one way to do things

+ act how you wish others would act when you are leader

+ be a team player

+ encourage the rest of the team to follow the leader

+ set an example by fully cooperating with the leader and doing what the leader asks, needs or expects

+ don't second-guess the leader

+ usually keep your mouth shut – even when you think the leader might be making a mistake

+ keep a positive attitude and avoid negative thoughts, words or actions

+ be "obedient," "loyal," "helpful," "friendly" and "cheerful"

+ be available to the leader as a resource but do not push your views on the leader.

We Scouters need to be good followers too. The Patrol Method demands it. If you delegate authority to a Patrol Leader, don't try to take that authority back.

Leave it where it is unless there is a compelling reason. We should be ready and willing to give advice or constructive criticism – especially when a moral or ethical issue arises. However, it is usually better to do this in a way that will not undercut the Patrol Leader's authority or confidence.

We Scouters can find it especially difficult to let a Patrol Leader make what we are sure is going to be a mistake. We want "to get in there and tell them how to do it right." But sometimes, what we think is a mistake turns out not to have been a mistake at all – just a different way of doing it. Other times, we will be right about the mistake, but it can be better to let the Scout with the leadership responsibility make the mistake and learn from it.

> **Baden-Powell said:**
>
> "[I]t is just by making mistakes that a boy gains experience and makes his character."

Leadership Yarn

Crew 812-A was triumphant - they had made it to the top of Black Mountain! It had been tough caterpillaring up all those switchbacks, but the view from the top was spectacular. When it came time to descend to Black Mountain Camp, the Crew's "Naviguesser" used his compass to figure out which of two trails to take. He took one he thought was right and began hiking down the steep incline. The entire crew followed with the Adult Advisors at the rear.

After awhile, the "trail" from the summit seemed to peter out. "What kind of a trail is this?" asked one Scout as he stepped over deadfall. "Where do we go from here?" Philmont's trails, while unblazed, are usually very distinct. This was no trail – it was a runoff stream bed!

The Scouts stopped, sat down, pulled out their topographic map and oriented it with their compass. They could not tell where in the world they were. Crew 812-A was temporarily misplaced on a steep mountainside in a remote part of South Country.

Adult Advisor Fitzpatrick took out a small inexpensive GPS unit. In a few moments, the GPS had picked up signals from a network of satellites orbiting the earth about 20,000 km above him at 14,000 km/hour and announced that it was "ready to navigate." The GPS's small screen was now displaying (using the NAD83 map datum) the Crew's current position down to 10 or 20 meters in accuracy. By plotting the UTM grid coordinates on the map, it became immediately apparent that the Crew had bushwacked down the wrong side of Black Mountain and were nowhere near the trail.

"Mr. Fitzpatrick," said the Crew Leader. "Did you know we were off the trail?"

"I thought something was amiss when we had to climb over all those logs," Fitz replied, shrugging his shoulders with a twinkle in his eye.

"Why didn't you tell us?" inquired a Crew Member.

"It's your crew," Fitzpatrick answered. "You are all trained in map and compass. I'm just along for the ride."

A lengthy discussion about what to do next ensued. Fitzpatrick, who was staring at the map, kept quiet. Finally, when the Scouts seemed to have run out of ideas, Fitzpatrick suggested "Well, we could go around."

"What do you mean?' asked the Naviguesser.

"I mean we could follow our contour line around the mountain to the west," said Fitz. "Go neither up nor down. We will eventually intersect the trail."

That's precisely what the Crew set about to do. The Scouts began following compass bearings around the mountain while maintaining constant elevation. Forty-five minutes later, after crossing some boulder fields and avoiding one steep dropoff, Crew 812-A had successfully bushwacked around the mountain to the Black Mountain Camp trail. The crew cheered. Not long thereafter, they were enjoying the cool water of Urraca Creek and getting ready to shoot black powder rifles.

Should Assistant Scoutmaster Fitzpatrick have allowed the Scouts to make this mistake? Suppose the crew was low on water or a storm was approaching? What if Fitzpatrick had not been carrying a GPS with fresh batteries so the risk of getting truly lost increased? Suppose the terrain had been more treacherous? These are the kinds of judgment calls any Scout leader must make all the time. If health and safety is a factor, then you likely want to step in and prevent a mistake. Otherwise, it may be best to allow the Scouts to fail safely and learn from their mistake.

Sharing Leadership through Consensus

A leader of a Scout troop should try to get general agreement whenever he can. After all, a Scout troop is a volunteer organization that runs based on shared leadership. But seeking consensus is not always appropriate. Margaret Thatcher once said, "consensus is the absence of leadership." Ms. Thatcher went on: ""Ah consensus … the process of abandoning all beliefs, principles, values and policies in search of something in which no one believes, but to which no one objects; the process of avoiding the very issues that have to be solved, merely because you cannot get agreement on the way ahead. What great cause would have been fought and won under the banner 'I stand for consensus'?"

Some Scoutmasters want everyone to like them. This type of leader has trouble directing others. His other difficulties may include:

- overly considerate of everyone's opinion about what should be done – even if he thinks some of their ideas are counterproductive or worse

- unable to set meaningful priorities

- always seeks approval from superiors, subordinates and anyone else who is willing to offer an opinion

- a great compromiser who tends to cave in to demands of others

- afraid or unwilling to take a hard line – even on important issues – because he's afraid somebody might not like him

- can not be objective about what is to be accomplished

- might be likable but is more likely pitied.

Decisions based on consensus can be ruled by strong individuals with strong self-interest. Individual self-interest is often not the same as what is actually best for the group as a whole. For example, simply because most Scouts (or parents) do not want to be troubled with fundraising does not mean that the Troop should not raise funds. What about the self-reliance that fundraising teaches the Scouts? What about the Scout families who cannot afford to write big checks for summer camp or Philmont?

Sometimes a leader has to stand up and lead courageously in a direction he thinks is right for the group – even if that direction is unpopular. A good leader must sometimes trade off getting buy-in from most of the group with doing the right thing and leading the group in the right direction.

Sharing Leadership by "Joining In"

Every now and then, Scouts or even Scoutmasters may want to stop being the leader and instead join in and become part of the group. They need to understand that by ceding all authority to the group, they will lose control. There may be some limited situations where this is appropriate. For example, when playing games that do not require a leader, the Patrol Leader might be tempted to become "one of the guys." He should be careful. New leaders who are not yet comfortable with a leadership role sometimes unintentionally give up control to the group and then cannot get control back when they need it.

Leadership Yarn ~~~~~~

Jack, the Patrol Leader of the Bobcats, was trying to get his Patrol to break camp so the Troop could get back on the trail. Scott and Tony were playing around with sticks instead of taking down their tents. Jack went over to tell Scott and Tony to stop the horseplay. But Jack loves a good stick swordfight, too, He soon became engaged in a three-way stick fight. Daring jabs, hiding behind trees – just like the Three Musketeers! Before Jack realized, the Senior Patrol Leader had come over and wanted to talk to him. The rest of the Troop was ready to get back on the trail. The Bobcats had yet to strike their tents.

Evaluating Leadership

Reading this section has likely reminded you of different leaders you have experienced (or sometimes even been yourself) and experiences you have had as a leader or follower. Some leadership styles are more effective than others. Some styles do not work at all. The most effective leadership styles are the ones that come from the heart.

A good leader adjusts his leadership style to fit the situation. Effective leaders also adapt their leadership style to fit the collection of people they are leading at the time as well as group dynamics.

When we lead, we influence our followers with our own style of leadership. When we train a Scout to lead, we are instilling a part of our own leadership style into that Scout.

A Scout Troop cannot function without shared leadership. Shared leadership is the key to effective leadership training. Delegation must be done thoughtfully and carefully. It is important to not delegate beyond a Scout's abilities. You want to set the Scout up to succeed, not fail. You also don't want to relieve a Scout of authority delegated to him unless this is essential to group success.

As Patrol Leaders lead their Patrols through different situations, they should not be afraid to try out different leadership techniques. Each person should see what works for him and what does not by evaluating his performance and the performance of the group he is leading.

Candid Self-Evaluation and Self-Assessment

"The aim of leadership is not merely to find and record failures in men, but to remove the causes of failure."
— W. Edwards Deming

It is human nature to gloss over or ignore our own weaknesses and focus on our strengths. More often than not, "recognition" is the watchword in a volunteer organization such as the Boy Scouts. Many in volunteer organizations feel it is easier to pretend problems do not exist and that every test has been passed with excellence. Criticism is negative, but we all want to be positive. Parents will not rest until their son has received every bit of the credit and recognition he so richly deserves.

It is up to us to provide effective mechanisms our Scouts can use to measure and realistically evaluate their own leadership skills – as well as ours. Healthy inter-Patrol competition provides one very direct form of objectively assessing leadership. Candid feedback in the form of mentoring and counseling can also help leaders assess their own strengths and isolate areas they need to improve upon. We encourage you to teach and follow the BSA's "Start, Stop, Continue" leadership assessment tool which provides a non-threatening way to assess team progress. This applies to your own leadership execution as well as to what your Scouts are doing.

Experienced leaders know that candid self-assessment is itself a crucial leadership skill. Socrates advised: "Know yourself." Effective leaders know how important it is to evaluate their own performance. A leader who is realistic about his own capabilities is confident but also ready to seek help and advice in areas other than his strengths.

Those dedicated to Scout-led shared leadership models understand that evaluation ought to be a shared responsibility to be conducted by the group – not just the Scoutmaster. Since the Scoutmaster sets the tone, his opinion is always very important. Nevertheless, the Scouts themselves can offer excellent observations. Every PLC meeting should include some time for candid self-assessment. To be maximally effective, the Scoutmaster himself must be receptive to evaluation by the group.

Many Scout-led Troops and Crews have a tradition of "Roses and Thorns" discussions after each day or major event. Each participant is encouraged to tell what went right and what went wrong. The group listens to every comment without judgment. Each person's opinion matters and is valid.

Why not extend "Roses and Thorns" to leadership self-evaluation? The Patrol Leaders Council can assess how each leader is performing: "How am I doing as a leader?" Set the tone by creating an environment where leaders get honest answers and people are not afraid to say what they really think. This practice will build stronger leaders and a stronger team.

Techniques That Support the Patrol Method

Leadership Yarn

Assistant Senior Patrol Leader Bill believed he had well earned his green bars and paid his dues. He was tired of doing what other people told him to do. Now it was his chance to tell other Scouts what to do. Bill's first opportunity came during summer camp, when the Senior Patrol Leader was off at a Program Director's meeting and left him in charge of getting the Troop campsite ready for inspection.

Bill plopped himself down in a big comfortable camp chair in the middle of the campsite. Every now and then, he yelled an order to one of the Patrol Leaders. "Hey Bob! We got to get ready for inspection — get your Patrol to roll up tent flaps — and while you're at it, can your guys roll up my tent flaps, too?"

"Mickey, the Eagle Patrol is the Service Patrol today — get that latrine swept out right now!"

"Lou, get your guys to police the area, I saw all kinds of candy wrappers on the trail coming in," Bill yelled as he put his feet up on a log and leaned back.

When Bill did not get the cooperation he was looking for, he started getting frustrated and began yelling louder. "Hey you — Tenderfoot — what do you think you're doing? You are supposed to be policing the area, not sitting on your butt. Get going!"

"Bob, those tent flaps are still down, what's wrong with you guys!" Bill shrieked in frustration.

Just then, the Eagle Patrol came back from cleaning the latrine. The whole Patrol sat down around the campfire ring where Bill was sitting in his camp chair. Bill went ballistic. "What are you guys doing? Look at this campsite! The inspector is going to show up any time now! Get up out of those chairs and put that cooking stuff away."

Unfortunately, it was getting late. Scouts soon started leaving for merit badge classes. The campsite was still in disarray. Disgusted, Bill finally got up out of his chair, yelled "We're gonna get a lousy score on inspection — and it's gonna be your fault!" to no one in particular, and stomped off to his own merit badge class.

Later that afternoon, Bill ran into his Scoutmaster, Mr. Bergen, at the rifle range. "Mr. B., they just don't listen to me. I can't get these guys to do what they're supposed to," Bill complained. Bill started explaining how the Patrols did not clean up as he asked. "Maybe you can talk to them?" Bill asked hopefully.

Mr. B. listened carefully, and then asked Bill a question: "Bill, what were you doing at the time?"

"I was leading them — I was telling them exactly what to do," answered Bill proudly.

"You didn't answer my question," said Mr. B. "You told me what you were saying. I asked you what were you doing."

"Well, I guess I wasn't actually doing anything," Bill admitted. "I was sitting in my chair in the middle of the campsite where I could see everything and everyone. It's not my job to clean up the Patrol sites — I'm the leader."

"Bill, have you ever heard of 'show me' leadership?" asked Mr. B.

"Show me leadership?" asked Bill — who was now very interested in what Mr. B. had to say.

"What I mean," said Mr. Bergen "is that a leader's actions often speak louder than his words. By sitting back in your chair in the middle of the campsite where everyone could see you, your actions were telling everyone that it was okay to sit back, relax and take it easy. Your actions spoke louder than your words."

Bill thought about it for a minute, and realized that Mr. B. was right. For example, he remembered how the entire Eagle Patrol sat down right next to him instead of doing their work. "But I'm not supposed to do all the work myself, right?" asked Bill.

"No, you're supposed to get things done through the group, that's called the Patrol Method," said the Scoutmaster. "But you may have to show the other Scouts what you want them to do — not only to teach them how, but also to set the example. If they see you rolling up your own tent flaps, they will probably start rolling up their flaps too without you having to say a word. If they see you looking for litter on the ground, they'll probably start doing the same thing."

Leading by Example: "Show Me" Leadership

It was not too long ago when our sons first joined our Troop and became Scouts. Think back and remember how your son looked up to the older, more senior Scouts who were leading the Troop — the Patrol Leaders, the Senior Patrol Leader and the Assistant Senior Patrol Leaders. Those leaders worked with the new Scouts, guiding and helping them to learn the basic skills of Scouting. Most Scouts admire those older boys a lot — they want to act like them, talk like them and be like them.

Actions Speak Louder than Words

DO as you want others to DO
ACT as you want others to ACT
BE what you want others to BECOME.

Because of greater age, experience and elected office, the older Scouts are always "front and center" in the younger Scouts' eyes. Even when it seems as if no one is watching, the younger Scouts are always watching. Younger Scouts will copy what older Scouts do and follow their lead because they admire and look up to them — unless there is a good reason not to.

> **Baden-Powell said:**
>
> "Scouting is a game for boys, under the leadership of boys, in which elder brothers can give their younger brothers healthy environment and encourage them to healthy activities such as will help them to develop Citizenship."
>
> "You are living among your boys and are watched by each of them, and imitated unconsciously by them, and probably unobserved by yourself."

What an exciting opportunity — but what a big responsibility! Will our older Scouts set a good example or a bad example?

Leadership Yarn

Frank had just been elected Patrol Leader of the Red Hot Chili Peppers. Frank loved everything about Scouting — well, almost everything. The one thing he was not too crazy about was the uniform. Frank thought wearing khaki and green was embarrassing. "That neckerchief is so dorky! Definitely uncool," Frank thought to himself.

Frank found all sorts of excuses for not wearing his uniform to Troop meetings. Sometimes Frank would put on his uniform shirt just as he walked into the Troop meeting, but sometimes he did not even do that. He made excuses to the Senior Patrol Leader and the Scoutmaster — both of whom always seemed to manage to wear their uniform to nearly every meeting.

An interesting thing started happening in the Chili Peppers Patrol after Frank became their Patrol Leader. Even the totally gung-ho 11-year-olds in the Patrol started "forgetting" to wear their uniforms. Those same Scouts always had worn their uniforms before Frank became Patrol Leader.

Jerry was the one Scout in the Red Hot Chili Peppers who always wore his uniform. During Patrol Corners one troop meeting, Jerry asked the rest of the Peppers why nobody else was in uniform. Frank gave his usual excuse about baseball practice just before the Scout meeting. Gary, one of the younger Scouts, said "Well, Frank doesn't wear his uniform, why should I?" The rest of the Patrol members nodded their heads in agreement.

After the meeting that night, Frank started thinking about what Gary had said. Frank realized that the only way to get his Patrol back in uniform was for him to wear the uniform himself. Frank must set a good example. He could talk until he was blue in the face, but those younger Scouts were not going to wear their uniforms unless he did too!

At the next Troop meeting, Frank made a point of wearing his uniform. He even wore his green Scout socks — and he re-rolled his neckerchief several times until it was just right. That night, Frank wore his uniform with pride. He did not need to say a thing — you could tell by his body language and how he carried himself.

Now, it was the other Scouts' turn to be embarrassed — because they were not wearing uniforms! The following meeting, however, the Red Hot Chili Peppers Patrol got a 100% on uniform inspection — every member was in uniform.

The Senior Patrol Leader made a big deal out of congratulating the Chili Peppers in front of the whole Troop. Frank felt proud because he knew that his good example was the reason his Patrol won inspection.

> **Baden-Powell said:**
>
> "Personally, I put on the uniform, even if I have only a Patrol to inspect …. It is largely a matter of example. Show me a slackly-dressed Troop and I can 'Sherlock' a slackly-dressed Scoutmaster…. You are the model to your boys and your smartness will reflect itself in them."

We Scoutmasters set the stage for all Troop leadership to set a good example. We do this by setting the example ourselves. Of all the adults in the Troop, the Scoutmaster is the most visible. He is the adult leader to whom all turn. He cannot possibly expect his Scouts to do something he is not doing himself.

> **Baden-Powell said:**
>
> "There is no doubt whatever that in the boys' eyes it is what a [Leader] does that counts and not so much what he says… If you are lazy they will be lazy; if you make cleanliness a hobby it will become theirs…."

A leader can set the tone for the whole group. If he does not show much Scout Spirit, neither will the rest of the Scouts. If a leader refuses to sing at the evening campfire, there is no way the rest of the Patrol or Troop will sing. Scouts will pick up on negative messages or emotions immediately. Positive attitudes and enthusiasm, however, are contagious! Good Scouts inspire others to be the same.

Advancement: A Leadership Must

The Patrol Method uses the resources of the Patrol to accomplish an objective by working together. Advancement is the means by which Scouts develop better skills to support the Patrol Method. It makes them better team resources. It also provides them with the skill basis for training younger Scouts and thereby practicing their own leadership.

Patrol Leaders can be encouraged to create an environment that encourages learning and mastering of new Scouting skills. New skills mean capabilities will grow. Patrol Leaders need to understand the changing resources of the group to lead more effectively.

If Patrol Leaders Council members are behind on their own advancement, other Scouts will not take advancement seriously either. Advancement is sometimes an individual quest, but Patrol and Troop spirit and group effort can go a long way towards making sure everyone gets ahead together and has fun doing it.

Leadership Yarn

Summer camp in the Virginia foothills was always a treat for Troop 973. It was a week away from home and chores. It was camping out under the stars. It was all the merit badge classes and the waterfront activities. A favorite was watching the Virginia National Guard fly maneuvers around the lake. Summer camp was great!

This was Senior Patrol Leader Tad Roger's last summer camp before going off to college. He was a few months shy of his 18th birthday and was a Life Scout.

During rest time on the first day of camp, Scoutmaster Pitt asked Tad what he was doing about completing his Eagle requirements. After all, time was growing short.

"I figured I wouldn't go for Eagle but focus on helping the guys get their advancements instead," Tad offered.

"What! You're not going for Eagle?" Pitt was incredulous. "Over my dead boot you're not!"

Mr. Pitt was known for "encouraging" languishing Life Scouts to complete their work for Eagle. Truth be told, Mr. Pitt's parents had been in the military and moved from Europe to America just as he was approaching 18. He had been a Life Scout but he never got around to finishing his own Eagle. He was not going to let any of his boys who were that close not finish without a fight. Not on his watch.

"If you don't go for it, what are the younger guys going to think?" asked Pitt.

After further discussion, Tad finally gave in: "Okay, I'll give it a shot," Tad promised. Sure enough, Tad got it all done. The Troop had its first Eagle Ceremony in several years. All the other Scouts saw what it meant to become an Eagle. There were five more Eagle promotions in the next five years.

Some Scouts study advancement at home with their moms or dads. A parent's satisfaction in "helping" his or her son earn numerous ranks and merit badges is not, we feel, necessarily something a Scoutmaster should encourage. We believe it is better to do this in the Patrols. "Home advancement" is too much like Cub Scouts. It breaks down the tradition of older Scouts teaching younger Scouts through the Patrol Method. It is not right for a Scoutmaster to shut this down completely, but there are ways to encourage advancement within the Troop instead.

Building Trust

A primary quality of leadership is trust. Without it, no one can lead anybody to do anything.

A Leader Is Trustworthy

The first Scout Law says much of the essence of leadership. A leader must inspire trust in those he leads. He must also trust those whom he leads. Always be trustworthy and your leadership will be recognized. You will contribute to all the groups you are associated with throughout your life.

A leader cannot lead if he is not trusted. It is that simple. People will not follow someone they do not respect. Respect is earned from trust and establishing a track record of reliability, consistency and responsibility.

Trustworthy means more than not telling fibs and not cheating. It means following through and doing what you say you are going to do. It means being the "real deal" — a person with integrity whom people can always count on to do the right thing.

> **Baden-Powell said:**
>
> "Trust should be the basis of all our moral training."
>
> "The first Law, namely, a 'Scout's honour is to be trusted,' is one on which the whole of the Scout's future behaviour and discipline hangs. The Scout is expected to be straight."

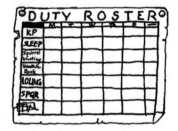

Everyone in the Troop knew that Larry, the Patrol Leader of the Vikings Patrol, and Mike, the Senior Patrol Leader, were good friends. They played on the same intramural basketball team and hung out together after school. Therefore, at summer camp, everyone noticed immediately when Mike began doing favors for Larry. Mike's duty roster gave the Vikings Patrol all the easy assignments. Mike never assigned the Vikings to clean the latrine, but he assigned the Bobcats latrine duty twice.

After the Bobcats grumbled, the Bobcat's Patrol Leader called Mike on it: "Mike," he said, "we don't think it's fair that we have latrine duty twice and the Vikings don't have it even once. Everyone should be treated the same."

At first, Mike was defensive. His friend Larry was carrying a heavy merit badge load — he wanted to make things easier on Larry so Larry could finish all those merit badges and catch up in rank. However, after thinking about it some more, Mike saw how helping his friend had hurt the trust that other Patrol Leaders had in him as a leader.

Mike finally decided the right thing would be to change the duty assignments to make them more even. He took down the old duty roster and posted a new one. He thanked the Patrol Leader of the Bobcats for letting him know how the Bobcats felt. When Larry asked Mike why he now was stuck with latrine duty, Mike explained: "Larry, I have to be fair. I've got to treat all the Patrols the same." Larry respected that decision.

Beware of Parental Conflicts of Interest

Many of us became adult leaders when our sons joined the Troop. As parents, we naturally want our sons to do well and distinguish themselves. But as Scout Leaders, we have responsibilities beyond being a good parent. When you wear the uniform of a Scoutmaster or Assistant Scoutmaster, you risk damaging your credibility and relationships of trust by showing favoritism to your own son. In your capacity as Scout Leader, you have not just one son in uniform but twenty or thirty. Beware of conflicts of interest. Do not be afraid to turn to other adults in your Troop to handle matters that individually affect your own son. Try not to brag about your son's accomplishments. Rarely if ever should you sign off on your own son's advancement. Be very careful at Troop election time. Above all, don't let your son try to use your authority to unfairly advance his own self-interests. Make it clear to him that you are there for him but also for the Troop as a whole.

Leadership Yarn

Mr. Timmons had just become Scoutmaster of Troop 1048. He and his son Kevin were chatting about the new arrangement. "I'm a sure shot for Patrol Leader now that you're the Scoutmaster, huh Dad," said Kevin enthusiastically.

"Not exactly," said Scoutmaster Timmons. Kevin looked puzzled. "What do you mean, Dad?" Kevin asked. "You told Mom you were volunteering for my sake."

"Kevin," said Mr. Timmons. "You know how much I love you. That is the very reason why I cannot play favorites. The other boys will not respect you if they suspect you got rank or office just because you are my son." Even though he knew it was a bit over the top, Scoutmaster Timmons decided to suggest an interesting approach to his son. "Kevin, why don't you try calling me every now and then 'Mr. Timmons' when we're around other Scouts in the Troop?"

"Mr. Timmons!?" cried Kevin. "C'mon Dad, gimme a break! Mom's gonna put a stop to that, she won't even believe you're suggesting it."

"Kevin, haven't you noticed how some of the other Scouts became less trusting of you when I became Scoutmaster? When we're with the Troop, let's see what happens if you call me what everyone else calls me: Mr. Timmons. In return, I'll call you Mr. Timmons."

Kevin was skeptical but agreed to try it after his father explained how it would help build up trust and credibility. Kevin was surprised at how his new attitude changed the way the other Scouts related to him. They no longer felt like he was getting ahead just because he was the Scoutmaster's son.

Giving Direction

The primary purpose of leadership is to provide direction. By providing direction, a leader is like a compass — he points the direction for his team to follow. Baden-Powell knew this well. He chose the fleur-de-lis because it was used on the old mariner's compass to indicate north, the direction to which all maps were and are oriented.

Direction Is the Primary Product of Leadership

Leaders see the horizon and direct others how to get there. They help identify what is to be accomplished and set the course.

Scouting builds leaders. Leaders show society direction. The three points of the fleur-de-lis represent the three fingers of the Scout Sign signifying duty to God and country, duty to others, and duty to self — all of which give Scouts direction.

Leadership Yarn

The Sting Ray Patrol was out on a hike. The Patrol stopped. There was disagreement on which direction to go. Some wanted to go on up the steep feeder trail along the ridge. Others wanted to bushwhack down by the stream. Still others wanted to stay on the main trail even though they believed this was the longest possible route to the campsite.

The Patrol Leader listened to the discussion ... for awhile. Finally, after hearing everyone's viewpoint, the Patrol Leader decided that everyone would stay together and follow the main trail. He did not necessarily need to decide all alone which route to follow — he also got everyone's input about the best route to take under the circumstances. The Patrol Leader explained his rationale: "The trail might be longer, but we're supposed to be practicing Leave No Trace. Besides, we won't get lost if we stay on the trail."

It is the leader's job to make the final decision and give clear direction so everyone in the Patrol stays together and follows the route.

We count on our leaders to have the vision to lead us with confidence and certainty to places we might not have gone to by ourselves. Think of Martin Luther King's "I have a dream" speech, or John F. Kennedy's speech that inspired missions to the moon.

Leading is *not* the same thing as managing. It has been said that leadership is doing the right thing whereas management is doing things right. Leadership provides vision and motivation, while giving followers real authority and control. The role of the Patrol Leaders Council is to inspire and lead, not to manage, the Troop. Similarly, the Scoutmaster should probably not try to manage the

Scouts in the Troop. Instead, the Scoutmaster's job is to have the vision to lead the way and effect change when needed. The role of a Patrol Leader is to lead and manage his Patrol. Collectively but individually, the Patrol Leaders manage the Troop.

Good Communication

Anyone reading a compass can see how the big red needle points to magnetic north. A leader must communicate direction just that clearly.

How many times have we been lost or made mistakes because we did not listen to directions? Experts in communications science tell us "communication takes place in the receiver." That means the "sender" must do whatever he can to make that reception clear and static-free.

Younger Scouts sometimes have short attention spans and are often so distracted that they do not pay attention. When giving directions to Scouts, the directions must be clear and easy to understand. Usually, it is best to communicate only one idea at a time. Sometimes it might help to draw pictures, make signs or write down notes or specific directions. We try to ask questions — we cannot assume they understand unless they respond. All effective communications must be two-way.

Leadership Yarn

Senior Patrol Leader Ted sometimes had trouble inspiring the Scouts in his Troop to do things but usually they would follow his lead. He tried to gain consensus when possible and found that persuasion was much more effective and respectful than intimidation, so he selected that as his leadership style. One thing that always eluded Ted was making others clearly understand his intentions and desires.

The Troop decided to climb Old Ragg Mountain one cool fall weekend. Freddy, Ted's next-door neighbor and fellow Troop member, resolved to pass his First Class cooking requirement. In those days, the First Class requirement read:

> "4.a. Camp Cookery — Prepare in the open, for yourself and a companion from raw ingredients, a complete breakfast of fruit, hot cereal and bacon-and-eggs (or griddle cakes); and a complete dinner of meat (or fish or poultry), vegetable, dessert and bread (or biscuits, or twist baked on a stick)."

> — *Handbook for Boys, 1950.*

"Fred, I'll be happy to serve as your tasting dummy so you don't poison anyone else!" Ted had joked. Freddy laughed. Ted walked away thinking Freddy had agreed that Ted would be Freddy's companion for the 1st Class cooking requirement.

On Saturday morning, everyone showed up at the meeting place, checked their gear and went to the trailhead to begin their hike up the steep trail. It took five hours with full packs and plenty of sweat — even with breaks each hour. They made it to the top and then found their campsite.

The sun was going down. Ted went up to Fred. "Well Fred, what are we dining on tonight?" Ted asked, thinking how lucky he was not to have carried all his food and cooking gear up that steep trail.

Fred smiled and said proudly, "I'm fixing beef stew from scratch, baked apple for dessert, some stick bread and Tang just like the astronauts drink in space. It'll be ready in about an hour, I think."

Ted finished setting up his tent and making sure the Patrols were doing well. He had really worked up an appetite and his stomach was growling. He was looking forward to hot beef stew.

Dinnertime came. Ted was front and center with his cup and utensils — much to Fred's astonishment. You see, there were two miscommunications on that trip. Fred had not read the First Class cooking requirement exactly as it was written in the handbook, so he missed the part about ". . . and a companion." He thought it was as Ted had previously indicated — just a tasting. Fred had brought only enough food for himself!

Ted had to get by on a few candy bars and crackers and whatever he could beg off others. After that, Ted never went unprepared again. Fred agreed he would have to pass the test on another trip.

Patrol Leaders should be the main conduit through which information flows between the Patrol Leaders Council and the members of their Patrols.

Leadership Yarn

All of the Patrol Leaders of Troop 873 attended Friday night's Patrol Leaders Council at the district camporee. One of the discussion topics was the campfire for the following night. The time of the campfire was set for 8 p.m. — right after church services. Tom, the Patrol Leader of the Bulls Patrol, volunteered his Patrol to do a skit at the campfire.

By the time Tom got back to the campsite, the Bulls were already in their tents. He joined the older Scouts drinking hot cocoa at the fire ring, and then went to bed himself.

By the next morning, Tom had forgotten all about the skit. He forgot to tell his Patrol at breakfast about the previous night's meeting and the upcoming campfire. Saturday was a busy day filled with Patrol competitions and games. By the time the Patrol got back to their campsite, it was already 5:00 p.m. and time to start cooking dinner.

During dinner, one Patrol member asked when the campfire was supposed to start. Tom suddenly remembered the skit. "Our Patrol is supposed to do a skit at the campfire!" he announced.

"How can we finish dinner, clean up, come up with a skit, and be at church services in full Class A's — all in less than an hour?" the Assistant Patrol Leader wailed.

The failure to promptly communicate basic information caused problems. The Patrol was surprised with information they needed to know earlier in the day. Nobody likes a surprise like that! After everybody calmed down, Tom got the Bulls to concentrate on coming up with a skit while cleaning up after dinner. The skit ended up being good because the Patrol got a chance to practice it while waiting for church services to start.

Most of effective communication is about *listening*. A Patrol Leader needs to *listen* to his Patrol members. A Senior Patrol Leader needs to *listen* to his Patrol Leaders. We all tend to love our own ideas. In a Scout-led Troop, however, it is the Scouts' own ideas that should count the most. Trust your Scouts to come up with good ideas. Listen to them carefully. Do not dismiss an idea just because you did not think of it yourself. We make it our credo that every Scout can have good ideas. Give your Scouts the freedom to control their own destinies and make Scouting their own.

Leadership Yarn

Assistant Scoutmaster Fitzpatrick agreed to mentor the Troop to raise a tower for a Scouting exhibition. Fitzpatrick encouraged Tom, the Senior Patrol Leader, to call a Patrol Leaders Council meeting to plan the construction. Fitzpatrick expected the Scouts to talk about tower design, training younger Scouts on proper lashings, and other logistics. He was surprised at the discussion which actually took place:

"Are we going to let kids climb the tower?" asked George.

"Of course," said Tom.

"What are they going to do once they get up there?" Brian asked.

"Look down," said George.

Tom got a big smile on his face and yelled: "And throw water balloons!"

The PLC became very excited about the idea of giving Scouts who successfully climbed the tower the ability to lob water balloons down onto those below. This was an idea that would never have occurred to Assistant Scoutmaster Fitzpatrick in a million years. It struck Fitzpatrick as not nearly so important as proper tower construction, but he did not squelch it. It was the Scouts' own idea and they were excited about it. Instead, he asked questions to guide them to do the advance planning needed to put their plan into action.

The day of the exhibition was hot and humid. After several hours of sweat and teamwork, the Troop raised a fine 12-foot hourglass tower. All day long, a constant stream of Cub Scouts wanted to climb the tower and throw water balloons down onto their Den Leaders. At the end of the day, SPL Tom walked up and said with a smile: "Mr. Fitzpatrick, that was the best Scouting event ever!" Fitzpatrick agreed: "It sure was fun watching those cubs throw water balloons down on their leaders. What a brilliant idea!" Tom's smile grew even wider.

We Scoutmasters need to communicate "The Why" and other important messages in clearly understandable ways. Lecturing teenagers is rarely effective. After we get the first five words out, we turn ourselves into the "blah blah-blah blah-blah" trumpet-sound of adults in a Charlie Brown cartoon. Storytelling is one way to break through and get your message across.

Storytelling: A Powerful Way to Communicate

We all have stories to tell. You do not have to be a professional storyteller. Throughout the ages, knowledge passed from family to family and generation to generation by telling stories around countless campfires. At Brownsea Island, Baden-Powell taught skills and lessons by carefully avoiding lectures and telling stories instead. Stories fascinate, they engage, and they are memorable. A powerful personal story can stay with the listener for a long time — sometimes even for a lifetime.

When do we Scoutmasters get opportunities to tell stories to our Scouts? All the time. Every Troop meeting. Every campout. Every campfire. Every Scoutmaster's Minute. Every announcement. Compare the following two announcements and see which one you think is more effective:

Announcement I:

I want to encourage everyone to attend our CPR training session this Saturday morning at 9 am. Knowing CPR is really important. You could save a life someday. It is not required for First Class, but it is required for First Aid Merit Badge and some of the water sports badges such as Rowing. It is not very hard to learn. It takes only a few hours. Practice is important. In the heat of the moment, you cannot be thinking about what you need to do, it has to be almost automatic. The Red Cross will be teaching us the skills we need to know. The Scout Oath tells us to help other people at all times. You need to know CPR if you want to be able to do that. I expect to see you all here bright and early on Saturday morning.

Announcement II:

Not long ago, in a small town in South Dakota, an off-duty airman of the United States Air Force was shopping in a grocery store when he saw a man let out a gasp and fall to the floor. The airman rushed to the man's side and asked the man if he was all right. The man was unresponsive. The airman put his ear near the man's mouth and found that he was struggling for every breath. The airman told a bystander to call 911. The airman put his finger on the man's carotid artery [demonstrating] and found a weak pulse. Within seconds, the man stopped breathing. The airman then did what he had been trained to do — he began CPR immediately. He did not have time to think about what he was doing. He just reacted based on his training. The man began breathing again. The paramedics soon arrived. The man's life was saved. The airman said he did what he did because of the CPR training he received each year in the Air Force. He said he would not have known what to do had it not been for that training. You too can be trained to save a life. Be here at 9 am on Saturday morning to learn how. I hope to see you then.

Stories are all around us. They are in the newspapers, on the Internet, in *Boy's Life* magazine, in the history books, in movies and on television, and in the everyday life of a Scout Troop. We mine these stories for effective ways to get our messages across. We are not concerned that we are not professional storytellers and cannot make people laugh or cry with our stories. Effective communication is an essential leadership skill. We have become more effective storytellers with practice. Soon it becomes second nature. Your Scoutmaster's minutes will be more compelling, your announcements will be more effective, and your Troop campfires will be more interesting.

Logical and Consistent Decisionmaking

Before a leader can give clear direction, he must decide what direction to take. Good leadership requires accurate and effective decision-making. A leader must provide the right conditions for good decision-making.

Decisions Are Best Made at the Lowest Level

Decisions should be made by the people who are most directly affected by them. In Scouting, that is usually at the Patrol level first and at the Patrol Leaders Council second.

Few leaders have all of the answers. They need input from others — from those they lead. Patrol Leaders need input from their Patrol Members. The Patrol Leaders Council needs it from the Patrol Leaders and sometimes from the Scoutmaster as well. Scoutmasters need input from the Patrol Leaders Council and the other adult leaders and from the Troop Committee.

Leadership Yarn ～～～～～～～～～～～～～～～～～～～～～～～～～～～～～～～～～～～～～～～

The Patrol Leaders Council decided the Troop would take a backpacking trip in March. It decided to hike through the woods for at least 10 miles, and camp overnight far away from any town. The older Scouts were thrilled at the prospect. In deciding on this plan, however, the Patrol Leaders Council failed to take into account that by March the Troop would have many new Scouts who just bridged over from Cub Scouting.

The new Scouts could hardly wait to go on their first Boy Scout camping trip, but they had never been backpacking before. They did not have the proper equipment or skills. Most of them were not up to the physical demands of a difficult trek through the backcountry. Some of the new Scouts were not quite yet ready to go camping without their parents, but the parents were intimidated by the idea of backpacking.

The new Scouts and their parents started grumbling. "What kind of a Troop plans its outings so only half the Scouts can go?" they complained.

Just when it looked as if the whole trip was ready to fall apart, an adult leader decided to try to help by coming up with a compromise: "Instead of going into the backcountry," he said, "let's go on a training hike along country roads and camp in a farmer's field. That way, the new Scouts and their parents can come along by car if they want, and you older Scouts can use the trip to train for a real backcountry venturing trek we can take this summer."

This sounded like a great idea to the new Scouts and their parents — but the Troop's older Scouts were less than thrilled. They had their hearts set on a backcountry trek. They resented an adult overruling their decision.

The result was quite predictable: older Scouts suddenly found they had other things to do that weekend. Only the younger half of the Troop went on the training hike. With much of the Troop's leadership opting out, the Patrol Method fell apart and the outing ended up being led by adults instead of Scouts.

The unsatisfactory outcome described above could have been avoided had decisions been made at the right level. The Patrol Method totally fell apart when the adult leader tried to help by taking over the decision. If decisions had been made at the lowest level, the result might have been a two-tiered outing. For example, the older Scouts could have hiked in to meet younger Scouts at an accessible campsite just off a hiking trail. Perhaps there could have been two different Troop outings that month.

Making decisions at the lowest possible level is important but it is also important that the right decision makers make good decisions. How do you make good decisions and avoid making bad ones? There are ways to improve decision-making and avoid making mistakes. For example:

* **Take time.** Start, stop, continue. Stop, think, and collect your thoughts and focus. Even in an emergency, there is usually enough time to take a few deep breaths, count to 10 and think. For longer-term decisions, "sleep on it" and let your subconscious mind work while you sleep.

* **Consider all alternatives,** but trust your gut. Much of good decision-making depends on experience, so do not ignore your instincts.

* Do not be afraid to **ask others** for advice or information. Often, "two heads are better than one."

- **Organize your thinking.** Some people write down lists of "pros" and "cons" to help them make a decision. Others talk out the problem with another person who acts as a sounding board.

Effective leaders come to understand that making good decisions is something that requires learning by doing. It takes a lot of practice and experience and often making mistakes along the way. Scouting is an ideal place to get this kind of experience. The entire Scouting program is designed to give Scouts a lot of responsibility so they can make mistakes in a safe way and learn from those mistakes.

Setting Priorities

Not all decisions are equal — some decisions are more important or should be made sooner to get the job done. Leaders must learn how to set priorities and be flexible enough to change them as situations shift.

Decide What Is Most Important and Act on It

Not everything can be done at once nor should it be. Leaders need to set priorities and follow them until situations change and require changed priorities.

Leadership Yarn

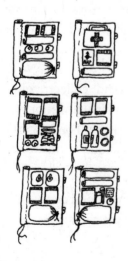

Tenderfoot Bob's second Scout campout was a backpacking overnighter along the Appalachian Trail. The fall leaves were changing colors and the weekend forecast was clear and cool — a perfect backpacking weekend.

Bob thought he understood what it meant to "Be Prepared" — just bring everything you might need. He carefully packed as much stuff as would fit into his new backpack, including his trusty Scout Handbook which he tucked into the top flap of his pack so he could easily refer to it.

At the trailhead, Bob lifted his backpack onto his shoulders for the first time. "This isn't so bad," he thought to himself. But by the end of the first mile up the steep trail toward the summit of Mohawk Mountain, Bob's shoulders ached and he was so winded he couldn't keep up. He plopped himself down alongside the trail. He felt ready to give up. He had not expected backpacking to be so hard!

Bob's Scoutmaster was soon sitting beside him. "How's it going?" Mr. W. asked him as he took off his left hiking boot and adjusted his sock to prevent hot spots from developing. "Not so well," Bob replied. "I don't think I'm ready for backpacking."

Mr. W. put his boot back on and tied it. "Well," he said, "let's check your pack, maybe we can redistribute the weight a little." Bob opened his pack and started pulling out all sorts of stuff — including that trusty Scout Handbook.

"Why did you bring this?" asked the Scoutmaster, holding up the handbook and trying hard to keep a straight face.

"Thought I might need it," Bob said meekly and more than a little embarrassed, his face turning as red as the Fall maples in the tree canopy above him.

"Bob," the Scoutmaster said, "on a backpacking trip you can't bring everything — you have to prioritize. You take only the stuff you really need. After your ten essentials, anything you bring on a backpacking trip that you don't end up using is probably something you should have left at home."

Mr. W. offered to carry Bob's Scout Handbook in his own pack, and got a few of the older Scouts to carry some of Bob's other "extra" items — after all, those older Scouts had neglected to do a new Scout gear shakedown back at the trailhead.

With his lightened load, Bob was able to finish the hike, exhausted but triumphant — and having learned a hard lesson about what it means to prioritize. The older Scouts learned a valuable lesson too; do the gear shakedown before the trip.

Logic and Consistency

We have already seen that trust is a major ingredient of leadership. Without it, you simply cannot lead. Two other things will help build trust in your leadership: logic and consistency.

Be Logical and Consistent

Leaders build trust when they demonstrate their leadership is predictable, measured, logical and consistent.

Leadership Yarn

"I never could figure out what Dan wanted," the first Patrol Leader sighed, talking about a former Senior Patrol Leader.

"Yeah," the second Patrol Leader agreed. "Everything would be okay with him one minute; the next minute he would make us change it all around. Sometimes I thought he was just on a power trip, making us do work for no reason at all."

"Remember the time he told us to get ready for a hike at Big Meadows? Then 10 minutes later, he told us to forget about the hike and start making dinner instead?" the first Patrol Leader complained. "Boy did my Patrol get mad! I asked Dan the reason why — he just said 'Cause I said so!'"

"I don't think he was trying to mess with us. I think he just didn't know what he was doing," the second Patrol Leader commented. "Then he would try to cover it up by making it sound like he planned it that way all along. He tried to make it seem like he was just testing us — except there was no rhyme or reason to it. You never knew what to expect from the guy."

Consistency is just as important to strong leadership. A good leader can be counted on to make decisions and lead in a manner that minimizes surprises and uncertainty. For example, if leaders always follow through with outing plans and go on the activity, they are acting in a consistent manner. The Scouts can believe that when they arrive at the appointed time they will actually be able to go to the event. If people are going to be led, the leadership decisions must make sense to them.

Representing the Team

A Scout Troop is democracy in action. Each Patrol elects its own Patrol Leader, and the whole Troop elects the Senior Patrol Leader. The Patrol Leaders Council is a little like the United States Congress. Each Patrol Leader represents the interests of his Patrol to the Troop at large just like senators from our 50 states.

Represent Your Team

Before the Patrol Leaders Council and the Troop, the Patrol Leader pushes for his Patrol's needs and interests.

When a Patrol Leader gets to the Patrol Leaders Council, his job is to "represent" his Patrol. This means the Patrol Leader should not push just for what he wants personally. Instead, he represents the needs and wants of all the other members of his Patrol. Doing this conscientiously is part of the responsibility of being a Patrol Leader or any other leader with a constituency.

The Patrol Leaders Council represents the Troop to the Scoutmaster staff and Troop Committee. The Senior Patrol Leader provides a summary of the Patrol Leaders Council's actions and the needs of the Patrols and the Scouts that comprise them. It is important to include this representation in the decisions that leaders throughout the Troop make.

Baden-Powell said:

"The Patrol Leaders Council ... is an important part of the Patrol System. It is a standing committee which, under the guidance of the Scoutmaster, settles the affairs of the Troop, both administrative and disciplinary. It develops in its members self-respect, ideals of freedom coupled with a sense of responsibility and respect of authority, while it gives practice in procedure such as is invaluable to the boys individually and collectively as future citizens."

For example, the older Scouts in the Troop may have already had their share of car camping, and may be yearning to go on high adventure outings instead. Nevertheless, a Patrol Leader cannot think only about himself and buddies his own age. A Patrol Leader also needs to think about every member of his Patrol. The younger Scouts will not likely be ready for high adventure yet. Their needs should also be considered.

> **Baden-Powell said:**
>
> "If I were asked what is the prevailing vice in the world I should say —
> Selfishness... The Scouting practices tend in a practical way to educate
> the boy out of the groove of selfishness."

What if the Patrol Leader does his best as an advocate for the Patrol's interests before the Patrol Leaders Council, but the Patrol Leaders Council decides to do something else? Sometimes a Patrol Leader may find himself having to "sell" the PLC's decision to his Patrol. This too is part of the Patrol Leader's job.

Leadership Yarn

Before the Patrol Leaders Council held its annual planning meeting, Patrol Leader Tyrone asked his Patrol (the Condors) what they wanted to do for the Troop's big fall outing. Everyone in the Condor Patrol wanted to kayak down the river and camp overnight on an island. Tyrone presented this idea at the Patrol Leaders Council meeting and argued for it. Not everyone agreed.

The Bobcat's Patrol Leader was worried about non-swimmers in his Patrol not being able to participate. The Quartermaster was concerned about the cost of renting kayaks. Somebody else was concerned about insects on the water. The Patrol Leaders Council voted. Tyrone voted for kayaking on behalf of the Condors, but backpacking won. Tyrone was disappointed. He knew the rest of the Condors would be too.

When Tyrone next met with his Patrol, his job was to "sell" the backpacking trip. Instead of complaining about not being able to go kayaking, Tyrone had to get the rest of the Condors excited about going backpacking. The Patrol Leaders Council voted and made the decision, so it was now Tyrone's responsibility as Patrol Leader to stand behind that decision and make it a successful trip.

Tyrone has another leadership opportunity as a result of the PLC's decision. He can organize a Condor Patrol kayaking trip as a Patrol outing, and arrange for proper adult supervision. However, Tyrone must be careful that the Condor's kayaking trip does not undercut the Troop's backpacking trip. It is important for Tyrone to make sure the Patrol Leaders Council understands that the kayaking trip is a Patrol outing but not a protest of the Patrol Leaders Council decision. In fact, Tyrone could have offered this solution at the Patrol Leaders Council meeting, had he thought of it then, and invited other older Scouts who were interested to attend as well.

Getting Input from the Team

A Patrol Leader should ask his Patrol for ideas before going to Patrol Leaders Council meetings. How can he represent them if he does not ask them what they want and need?

Sometimes, a Patrol Leader does not have a chance to get his Patrol's input before making a recommendation to the PLC. The Patrol Leaders Council might have to decide on something the Patrol Leader does not expect in advance. To make a recommendation without asking his Patrol first, the Patrol Leader must know each member of his Patrol well enough to be able to predict how he would feel about the issue. The Patrol Leader must know each patrol member's capabilities as well as his likes and dislikes.

Leadership Yarn ⚞⚞

Troop 624 was planning a big feast one night at summer camp for everyone including the parents. Each Patrol was going to cook a different dish. The Patrol Leaders Council met beforehand to decide on a menu. Before the Patrol Leaders Council meeting, each Patrol Leader asked his Patrol what food they wanted to prepare.

The Burning Pants Patrol told Johnny, its Patrol Leader, that it wanted to cook gumbo for the feast. One of the Patrol members was originally from Louisiana, and his mother had taught him how to make gumbo. At the Patrol Leaders Council meeting, the PLC realized that there would be too many main courses. Johnny could not ask his Patrol what to do — he needed to decide by himself how to handle the situation. To save his Patrol some work, Johnny volunteered that his Patrol would make a side dish instead of a main course.

What Johnny did not take into account was that the boy from Louisiana was dying to make his family's special gumbo for the entire Troop. When Johnny got back from the Patrol Leaders Council meeting announcing that he had saved his Patrol work by not having to make a main dish, everyone was disappointed. If Johnny had known the interests of his Patrol better, he would have made a different decision.

A compromise Johnny might have been able to suggest could be to ask another Patrol Leader if his Patrol would be willing to make a side dish instead of a main course. If so, then the Burning Pants Patrol could start their Cajun cooking tradition. If not, there is always the next trip. The Patrol Leaders Council can consider this culinary resource at that time.

Effective Teaching

Part of a leader's responsibility is to teach others. Teaching does not necessarily need to be like school — in fact, a great way to teach is through a two-way conversation rather than by lecturing. The BSA trains on the Teaching EDGE™. Another good way to teach is to let the learner discover on his own why he needs to know the lesson. This is called "self-discovery." The learner is given a chance to immediately use the newly learned skill.

Be an Effective Teacher

It is not enough for a leader to know how to do things himself. His job is to teach his knowledge to others. The team will be more effective if everyone knows all of the important skills.

Leadership Yarn

Troop Instructor Ed volunteered to teach new Scouts the bowline knot. Before the Troop meeting, he practiced the bowline so he could tie it one-handed with his eyes closed. Also before the meeting, Ed got enough rope from the Troop Quartermaster so each new Scout could practice.

Ed assembled the new Scouts in a corner of the meeting room. He told Jose, a new Scout, to imagine he was standing on a rock ledge 15 feet below the edge of a cliff. Ed said, "Jose, you have just fallen off the cliff and were lucky enough to land on this ledge. You need to be rescued."

Ed threw Jose one end of a rope and said, "Okay, here's a lifeline. Tie this rope to yourself so we can all pull you up off the ledge."

Jose had no idea how to safely tie a rope to himself. He tried using two half hitches but immediately realized that this knot would not work and might be dangerous because the knot could slip and tighten around him. Ed said "Okay, Jose, now I am going to show you how to tie a bowline knot you can use to save a life."

After making a "self-discovery" that he did not have a clue how he would tie the rope to rescue himself, Jose was now really interested in learning how to tie the bowline.

Ed showed Jose and the rest of the new Scouts how to tie the bowline. He had enough ropes so each new Scout could immediately practice it a few times.

After the practice session was over, Ed told the new Scouts to return to their Patrols. Ed then set up a game for the whole Troop using the bowline. Ed asked each Patrol to send one of the new Scouts in the Patrol to the far end of the room. The Patrol member sat on a piece of cardboard. The rest of the Patrol had to throw a rope to the new Scout. The new Scout sitting on the cardboard had to tie the rope around himself using a bowline. The Patrol would then pull the new Scout across the room by pulling on the rope. The first Patrol to cross the finish line would win.

> **Baden-Powell said:**
>
> **"We found the best way of imparting theoretical instruction was to give it out in short instalments with ample illustrative examples when sitting round the camp fire or otherwise resting ... The practice was then carried out in competitions and schemes."**

This form of teaching was exactly what Baden-Powell employed at Brownsea Island. His teaching method had three steps, which still work today:

* first, instruct and practice
* second, make a game of the lesson
* third, teach another Scout.

This is entirely consistent with modern BSA leadership training principles of Teaching EDGE™ (Explain, Demonstrate, Guide, Enable). One of the best ways to learn is to teach. A Scout will remember a skill he has to teach to another Scout.

Leadership Yarn

Life Scout Owen Rader was embarrassed. The Woodcarving Merit Badge counselor had taken his knife away because he had cut himself too many times trying to carve a neckerchief slide. The Counselor told Owen he could get his knife back *only after another Life or Eagle Scout retested him on second class Toten' Chip requirements.*

Scoutmaster Durbin went to talk to the Counselor. "Owen is a little embarrassed about having to ask another Scout to teach him basic skills. What if we ask Owen to teach a younger Scout Toten' Chip? He will probably learn more by teaching," Durbin proposed. The Counselor readily agreed.

The same is true for teaching leadership skills. The Scouting program is designed for new Scouts to learn from older Scouts. Likewise, new leaders will learn from more experienced leaders. This is another reason why leaders should be careful to remember that others are watching everything they do. Much leadership is learned by observing people we trust and admire.

Own Your Leadership

Ownership is an important element of leadership. Followers must understand that their leaders clearly own the direction they give.

Own Your Leadership

Credible leaders "own" their leadership. They have responsibility and they decisively exercise it. They take their work seriously and they stand behind their decisions.

Leadership Yarn

During a Scoutmaster Conference with Brian, a young Scout seeking promotion to Life, Scoutmaster Bergen determined that the young man was not sufficiently experienced in leadership to be ready for promotion. He had not yet served as a Patrol Leader, and had failed to demonstrate leadership in the Troop Historian position he had occupied. The Scout was crestfallen. The parents were not too pleased either.

The Scoutmaster owned his decision by explaining to Brian what he needed to do to remedy the situation. He suggested six months of monitored activity as a Troop Guide in First Aid. Over the intervening months, he would be able to observe Brian and his leadership in organizing and teaching Tenderfoot, Second Class and First Class first aid.

When Brian once again sought promotion, he and Scoutmaster Bergen discussed what Brian had learned about leadership and how it had made him a stronger candidate for Life Scout. Scoutmaster Bergen in owning his decision did Brian, and the Troop, a great service.

The Scouting program is not a "pass/fail" system. Nor is it a matter of competition. Scouting is an on-going opportunity to learn a body of knowledge that will serve the Scout well over his lifetime. We cannot all be good at everything, but we can learn a variety of helpful skills and leadership lessons during our time in Scouting.

Our work with the Troop is a continuum of achievement. In Scouting, every Scout has the potential to be a winner, whether or not he achieves Eagle Scout or Senior Patrol Leader. He is a winner because he learns things many of his non-Scout peers never will know. He improves himself and becomes stronger. Each Scout learns at his own pace. Probably the longest lesson for a Scout to learn is that of leadership. It literally takes years and is an ongoing process.

We encourage our Scouts to pace themselves and not attempt to complete the requirements for Eagle Scout too rapidly. Typically, they focus on the rank and merit badge skill requirements. If learned properly, these skills will stay with the Scout for a lifetime.

Nevertheless, the leadership skills are often more difficult and elusive. They require practice. Practice creates personal ownership.

Discipline: Encouraging Others to Do Their Best

Self-discipline is doing what you don't want to do when you don't want to do it.

Usually, discipline is associated with "forced direction." Instead of thinking of it in those terms, consider discipline as a focus of oneself. People who train for life-or-death situations, such as soldiers, police, first responders and firefighters, are said to be "well-disciplined" when they follow orders without question. "Charge Up that Hill!" orders the lieutenant, and the soldiers obey — even if it means the soldiers might lose their own lives by following the order. This type of forced discipline is critical in emergencies and in the military, but it is not appropriate in Scouting unless the situation is an emergency.

"They will never respect a commander who does not enforce discipline."

— Theodore Roosevelt, US President and Chief Scout Citizen

Baden-Powell spent his entire career in the British Army and was promoted to the rank of Lieutenant General. However, when it came to Boy Scouting, B-P's way of achieving discipline was to avoid using punishments and instead to encourage the individual Scout to be unselfish and self-disciplined.

Baden-Powell said:

"Insist on discipline and strict obedience... A nation to be powerful and prosperous must be well disciplined, and you only get discipline in the mass by discipline in the individual. By discipline I mean patient obedience to authority and to other dictates of duty. This cannot be got by repressive measures, but by educating the boy first in self-discipline and in sacrificing of self and selfish pleasures for the benefit of others."

In Scouting, instead of thinking about "discipline" as how to force someone to do something, we think of encouraging "self-discipline" that helps people to make good on their promise to do their best on their Scout's Honor. Discipline gives focus to the Scout's work and learning.

Baden-Powell said:

"The romance of the Knights has its attraction for all boys and has its appeal to their moral sense. Their Code of Chivalry included Honour, Self-Discipline, Courtesy, Courage, Selfless Sense of Duty and Service, and the guidance of Religion.

Sometimes new Patrol Leaders feel they must bark orders and threaten punishments to get things done. It might work for a time or two, but it soon fails and their "leadership" is rejected.

Leadership Yarn

Rodney served his Troop as a Patrol Leader for about a year. He was great at telling others what to do. He was even greater at supervising from his campstool.

The Patrol soon only did what was absolutely necessary. They resented his discipline of 20 push-ups for this "offense" and 10 laps around the camp for another so-called "offense."

At first, the Scouts thought it was funny. However, they soon came to see how Rodney was long on dishing out orders and punishment and short on inspiring them to do their best.

The annual Troop elections came around and Rodney wanted to serve as Senior Patrol Leader. He was a Life Scout looking forward to his Eagle project and wanted to show increasing leadership capabilities and experience. He knew that this would impress the National Board of Review when the time came for him to sit for his Eagle promotion.

Rodney's leadership skills had been demonstrated all too well in his capacity as Patrol Leader. His brother Scouts decided that they would prefer another Senior Patrol Leader candidate. Rodney was not elected. He was not even reelected to be a Patrol Leader. He held no office. He knew he'd have to explain this to the National Board as well.

In this yarn, had Rodney observed Baden-Powell's advice, he might have retained his position of leadership and earned the respect of his Troop. However, his fellow Scouts rejected his disciplinary style. When this happens, it is hard for a would-be leader to earn the respect and trust to receive again the opportunity and privilege to lead.

Rodney was perhaps not a "bad" Scout, but he was not a good leader. This jeopardized his future promotion to Eagle. It was also a tremendous blow to his ego. This experience was a good lesson for him, and an opportunity for his Scoutmaster to demonstrate some leadership as well.

Rodney was not elected because he used punishment as "leadership." He might have excelled at a special Scout skill and the Scoutmaster could make him a Troop Guide to teach that skill to the new Scouts. However, such an assignment cannot be to "cover" the Eagle leadership requirement. The assignment had to have substance, which the Scoutmaster could explain. Luckily, in Scouting, there are few career-destroying errors. Every Scout deserves a second chance.

Rodney's second chance was to learn from his mistakes and proceed with humility and service to others.

Praise and Recognition

There is an old saying: "Success breeds success and failure breeds failure." Good leaders praise accomplishments of their followers. They encourage success. They try to minimize failure by providing direction and monitoring results.

Praise Accomplishment and Success

One way to begin teaching leadership is to praise good leadership examples from other Scouts in the Troop. Encouragement can go a long way toward building the next generation of leaders.

Everyone responds well to praise. People want to be successful. Real leaders do their best to make that happen. However, it cannot be false praise or too freely given. Praise must be earned.

One way we do this in Scouting is through advancement. Scouts learn, succeed, and advance in rank and office. Another form of recognition is when a Scout demonstrates he is doing those things we normally associate with being a Good Scout.

Some Troops have a special "Scout Spirit" award they use to recognize this. It is awarded after the Troop votes for Scouts who have demonstrated they are Good Scouts. It can be a difficult decision because, unlike rank advancement, there are no specific requirements. Rather, the award is based on a general understanding that the selected Scouts have demonstrated that they live by the Scout Oath, Law, Motto and Slogan in their daily lives.

Leadership Yarn

One year at Scout camp, Jerry decided to master the bow and earn Archery Merit Badge. He was very frustrated and having a difficult time. Like all the shooting sports merit badges, archery requires some proficiency and much practice. Try as he would, Jerry just could not get it. His arrows flew everywhere except toward the clout!

About the third day, Scoutmaster Durbin, who was a bow hunter, stopped by the archery range and saw what was happening. He showed Jerry how to set his pull hand behind his jaw in exactly the same spot every time. He explained that it was much like the sights on a rifle, a merit badge Jerry had received the previous year. "Think of the arrow tip as the front sight and the placement of your pull hand behind your jaw as the rear sight," the Scoutmaster advised Jerry.

It worked! Jerry scored well and went on to be awarded the merit badge. But that's not the end of this yarn...

The following year, the camp's rifle instructor had his grandson in attendance for the summer. The grandson, Paulie, wanted to earn Archery Merit Badge. Scoutmaster Durbin and the rifle instructor had become good friends and enjoyed each other's company every year at camp. The instructor asked for the Scoutmaster's help. The instructor knew Scoutmaster Durbin was an archery merit badge counselor and bow hunter. He was sure Durbin could help his grandson.

Scoutmaster Durbin had another idea. After relating it, he gained the grandfather's approval.

"Hey Jerry, I need some help," Scoutmaster Durbin related.

"Sure thing Mr. Durbin, what do you need?" Jerry was always interested in helping because he was a friendly guy who really liked other Scouts and, if the truth be known, he also liked to show off what he knew a little bit too.

"You know Paulie, the rifle instructor's grandson?"

"Sure do, I saw him this morning."

"Well, he's having trouble with his archery. Seems he can't hit the broad side of a barn. His grandfather is great with a rifle but needs some help with the bow. I told him what a great job you did last year. Think you can help him out?"

Jerry took the young boy under his instruction. In a few days, Paulie too had mastered the bow well enough to earn Archery Merit Badge. When he did, the entire camp heard the pride of his accomplishment. Paulie was one happy camper! His grandfather was thrilled too!

The afternoon the young man qualified, Jerry saw Scoutmaster Durbin down near the mess hall. "Paulie made it! I showed him just what you showed me last year. It took us a few days, but he made it!"

Jerry was almost as excited as he had been when he qualified for the same merit badge himself the year before. "You know, I felt like a real leader today. It was real neat!"

At the Fall Court of Honor back at his Troop, Jerry was surprised to receive the Scoutmaster's Award. It was a newly carved hiking stick with his name on it. His role in helping the young boy earn the merit badge was told in detail to all present. It demonstrated not only how one Scout can teach another, but also how a Scout can learn the lessons of leadership and apply them to the next generation.

Jerry learned that success breeds success. He also learned that a little recognition could go a long way towards building a leader for the next generation of Scouting.

Leaders should always be thinking about how to use recognition and praise to inspire others to do their best. It is all too easy to criticize, but it takes practice to give praise. Give out awards often. They can be as simple as ribbons from the dollar store to hang on Patrol flags. Look for opportunities to tell others when they have done something well or have done their best. Even if their attempt was not a complete success, recognize the effort. Do not reward falsely, but be generous in handing out praise and recognition when it is well earned.

Leadership Yarn

At summer camp, Senior Patrol Leader Matt was upset at the Condor Patrol. Every time the Troop assembled for dinner, the Condor Patrol was the last Patrol to fall into line. Several times earlier in the week, Matt was on the verge of giving the Condors a tongue-lashing or getting the Troop to sing, "Here we sit like birds in the wilderness, waiting for the Condors to show." Each time, though, he was patient and held his tongue. Finally, Matt pulled the Condor's Patrol Leader aside on the way to the dining hall to talk about it. The Patrol Leader shrugged and told Matt he was doing the best he could. Matt was not pleased with the answer.

Assembly for dinner was in five minutes. Before calling the Troop to assemble, Matt decided to walk over to the Condor's campsite to see what was going on. Why were they always so late? What Matt saw amazed him. Every single member of the Patrol was busy cleaning up and organizing the Patrol campsite. Every tent was neat as a pin. Every firewater can was filled to the brim. The entire campsite was swept clean of debris. Now Matt knew why the Condors were always late — they were busy making their Patrol site the best in the whole Troop!

After observing the Condors in action, Matt returned to the flagpole and had the Troop bugler blow assembly. As usual, the Condors were the last Patrol to fall into line. As the Condors marched up, one of the other Patrol Leaders started making fun of the Condors, shouting "Here come the Condors, late again … did you break one of your wings?"

Matt quieted the Troop, and then called the Condor's Patrol Leader up to the front. The Patrol Leader came forward nervously, expecting a reprimand. Instead, Matt reached out, shook his left hand with his best Scout handshake, and said "Condors, I congratulate you for the cleanest, most organized Patrol site of the entire Troop. Thanks for all your hard work. Let's hear a big Troop cheer for the Condors!"

Jaws dropped throughout the other Patrols. Every member of the Condor Patrol got a big smile on his face, and the Condor Patrol Leader's smile was the biggest of all!

Celebrate Victories

One of the joys of Scouting is that victories abound. Scouts have lots of opportunities for victories though advancement, learning, competitions, doing good turns, and other activities. Victories are waiting to happen everywhere!

Good leaders use the occasion of victories to honor and recognize those they lead and encourage them to do more and participate fully. We do this in our Courts of Honor and during meetings with a good word about deserving Scouts.

Patrol Leaders Council members can do this more frequently. It means so much to the Scouts when their leaders recognize their victories. It encourages them to do more and learn more.

Celebrate All Victories, Large or Small

It is important to recognize victories both at the individual level and at the group level. Good leaders make every effort to recognize and celebrate victories.

Leadership Yarn ~~~~~~

Joey was a new Scout. He had never been a Webelos, but he really wanted to go camping. He had joined Troop 703 just the week before. Ken, the Patrol Leader of the Eagle Patrol, was assigned to teach Joey the square knot.

"Joe, it's just like tying your shoes, only instead of making what my little sister calls the bunny ears, you make another overhand knot instead," Ken explained. "The first overhand knot you tie right-over-left — like this" he demonstrated, "and, the second one you tie left-over-right — like this." Ken held up the finished square knot. "See how it looks like a square?"

Joey tried it, but he kept losing track of which rope end was "right" and which one was "left." He tied granny knot after granny knot. "Nope, that's not it," said Ken. "See how yours twists while mine makes a perfectly flat square?"

Ken had an idea. He went to the rope bag and found a length of red nylon line. He brought the rope back to Joey. "Okay, you can use this knot to join two ropes together. Now, start with the red end in your right hand. Right over left — that means you put the red end over the other one. That's it! See how the red end is now on your left? Now put the same red end over the other end again — left over right! That's it! Okay, now untie it and do it again all by yourself."

Joey did as Ken asked. He untied the knot, and then retied it. "Right over left ... and left over right" Joey said under his breath. He pulled the ends tight, and held up a perfect square knot.

"Yes!" said Ken. "Great job! See Joe, you're a Scout!" Joey was beaming. He had tied his first Scout knot.

If you were a Scout in your youth, you probably remember how it felt when you first mastered the square knot. Bet you wanted to show everyone you could do it, right? Well, it's the same for all new Scouts. It may seem like a little victory to you, but for them it's BIG! So celebrate it!

All accomplishments should be celebrated with a loud "attaboy!" By encouraging success, we build our Troops' strength and the leadership potential of those that follow. By celebrating victories, large and small, we make everyone feel great! Each victory celebration is like putting another log on the campfire of Scouting.

Create Your Personal Legacy of Leadership

Leadership Yarn ≈≈≈

The lights went dim. The audience fell silent. The honor guard proceeded down the aisle with the newest Eagle Scout at Post 106 that cool November evening. On the stage riser was a distinguished Scouter dispatched by Council to officiate. He had made Scouting his life's vocation and avocation. All of his peers in the Council respected him.

The new Eagle was feeling proud. Had he not completed all that was required? He had earned all the required merit badges, served leadership requirements as Patrol Leader, Senior Patrol Leader and JASM. He had been a Den Chief and Ordeal Master and Chapter Chief of his OA Chapter and had earned the God and Country Award and the Arrow of Light years before that.

He had done it all. Now, he was at the end of the Eagle Trail. However, the distinguished Scouter sensed all of this and would have none of it. He called for the recitation by the evening's honoree of the Scout Oath and Law for the auditorium attendees to hear. He administered the Eagle Pledge and Charge.

Then he told his signature story, which he saved for special ceremonies such as this one: "The Mountain Top Experience."

It was about a Scoutmaster who took his Troop hiking up a long and steep mountain trail. Along the way, many stopped to rest. Others turned back for camp. The rocks and impediments were too much for some. Some groused about the point of doing all this on such a warm day. However, the Scoutmaster just continued with anyone who would follow him.

Finally, he and just a few of the original hikers made it to the summit and enjoyed the view of what lay ahead. They experienced what the old man knew they would see — that there was no end to the trail. It just kept going on. As an Eagle, a Scout makes it to that summit and sees that there is no end. The trail simply continues.

The new Eagle got the message. He remained active in Scouting for a few more years, but daily commitments of work and family eventually forced him to hang up his uniform and put Scouting on a back burner. That is, until he had a son.

One day while they were hunting, the boy said, "Dad, I want to join the Scouts. My buddy John is joining the troop near our school and I would like to join too. But I'm having trouble with this thing they call the Scout Law."

"Well, I remember that. Let's give it a try." So all afternoon they spent time practicing the twelve points while they hunted.

Later that evening, they met the boy's mother and sister at a nearby restaurant. The boy wanted some coins to play the video games. "Before you do that, let's try that Scout Law one more time," his dad said.

The boy made the sign and began reciting. Typical of most new Scouts, he got "helpful, friendly, and courteous" all mixed up.

At that moment, at three separate tables in the restaurant, three different men made the sign they recalled so well from their youth. They helped the boy get through it. Four strangers who had never met became united in an old familiar brotherhood that the young man would soon discover for himself.

But that's not the end of the yarn either…

Years later, the father went on to earn his Wood Badge woggle and beads. The guest speaker at the final feast signifying the end of the outdoor practical of Wood Badge was a familiar if elderly gentleman, revered by all Scouters in his Council. His role as keynote speaker was to inspire the would-be Wood Badgers. They helped him to the podium. Once again, he told about "The Mountain Top Experience." It had been 28 years — or was it really only a few days? The old man and the Eagle Scout were reunited once again by the program they both loved.

We have gone almost full circle in our discussion of leadership.

Remember how we said in the beginning of this book that the mission of Scouting was to:

* serve others

* develop leadership

* have a lot of fun doing it.

Your leadership can do much to help the Scouts in your Troop achieve all this so your Troop grows and serves new Scouts to come.

Our legacy is the leadership we develop among the Scouts in our Troops to pick up our roles one day in their adulthood, serving as a Scoutmaster for a Troop somewhere. Therefore, our final learning lesson is:

Leave a Legacy of Leadership: Train Others How to Lead

The legacy of leadership is the leadership that is developed and left behind. Older Scouts train younger Scouts to be leaders so they in turn can teach still younger Scouts to come. It has been this way for a century. Without this legacy, leadership fails. With it, Scouting grows.

How do we leave a legacy? By giving others a chance to lead! Giving our Scouts and participating adults real responsibility and letting them lead creates the legacy. Leaving a legacy of leadership is perhaps the most important thing we Scoutmasters can do.

If each Scout leader doesn't train his successor, who will lead the Troop in years to come? If there is no one to lead the Troop, who will train the future leaders for our nation? If each Scoutmaster does not ensure that new leaders are trained, what will become of Scouting?

It's a circle. With a little luck, there will be a campfire in the middle of it!

Baden-Powell's Last Letter to Scouts

At 5:30 a.m. on the morning of January 8, 1941, Robert Stephenson Smyth Baden-Powell, Lord of Gilwell, died of a failing heart at his retirement home, Paxtu, in Nyeri, Kenya. He was almost 84. His final message to you and all other Boy Scouts was found among his papers:

To Boy Scouts

Dear Scouts,

If you have ever seen the play Peter Pan you will remember how the pirate chief was always making his dying speech because he was afraid that possibly when the time came for him to die he might not have time to get it off his chest. It is much the same with me, and so, although I am not at this moment dying, I shall be doing so one of these days and I want to send you a parting word of good-bye.

Remember this is the last you will hear from me, so think it over.

I have had a most happy life and I want each of you to have as happy a life too.

I believe that God put us in this jolly world to be happy and enjoy life. Happiness doesn't come from being rich, nor merely from being successful in your career, nor by self-indulgence. One step towards happiness is to make yourself healthy and strong while you are a boy, so that you can be useful and so can enjoy life when you are a man.

Nature study will show you how full of beautiful and wonderful things God has made the world for you to enjoy. Be contented with what you have got and make the best of it. Look on the bright side of things instead of the gloomy one.

But the real way to get happiness is by giving out happiness to other people. Try and leave this world a little better than you found it and when your turn comes to die, you can die happy in feeling that at any rate you have not wasted your time but have done your best. "Be Prepared" in this way, to live happy and to die happy — stick to your Scout promise always — even after you have ceased to be a boy — and God help you to do it.

Your Friend,

Baden-Powell

To Learn More

To learn more about leadership and leadership training, start with your fellow Scoutmasters. Sit down with them and talk about leadership. They will have lots to offer you.

We also recommend that you participate in your District or Council's Scoutmaster Leader Specific Training and Introduction to Outdoor Leadership Skills training programs. Then, sign up for Wood Badge training with your local council. Wood Badge can be a life-changing experience. It can make you passionate about the Patrol Method and passionate about your mission in Scouting.

We also recommend to you various publications of the Boy Scouts of America, including the following (available at the time this book was printed):

- *Scoutmaster Handbook*

- *Patrol Leader Handbook*

- *Senior Patrol Leader Handbook*

- *Boy Scout Troop Leadership Training Book & Troop Leadership Training Cards*

- *National Youth Leadership Training Guide & Memory Tip Cards*

- *National Youth Leadership Training Staff Guide*

- *Troop Program Resources (Games)*

- *Stages of Team Development chart*

- *Communicating Well DVD, No. AV-02DVD20*

- *Larson, John W., Youth's Frontier: Making Ethical Decisions: A Manual for Parents and Youth Leaders A Guide to Help Youth Meeting Today's Challenges (Boy Scouts of America 1985).*

- *Information on BSA National Website concerning "Youth Leadership Training Continuum"*

The following publications may also be helpful for further reading and research:

Robert Baden-Powell, *Scouting For Boys Reprint,* available from the BSA.

Robert Baden-Powell, *Aids to Scoutmastership*

John Graham, Outdoor Leadership: Technique, Common Sense & Self-Confidence (The Mountaineers, 1997) This book discusses leadership in the context of high adventure outdoor activities such as rock climbing but what it has to say about how to lead applies to all situations including Scouting.

Various Publications of The National Outdoor Leadership School (NOLS).

Various excellent publications from Project Adventure including *QuickSilver, Silver Bullets, Cowstails & Cobras II* (all available from www.pa.org)

"Green Bar" Bill Hillcourt, *Two Lives of a Hero* (Putnam 1964)

Jeal, *Baden-Powell* (Yale Univ. Press 2001)

Green Bar Bill Hillcourt's other writings about Scouting are pure gold — see, for example, the *Handbook for Patrol Leaders* (1950 Ed.), *The Handbook for Scoutmasters: A Manual of Troop Leadership* (BSA 1947) and the many essays in *Boys' Life* about Scout Leadership that Mr. Hillcourt wrote over the years.

Patrol and Troop Leadership (BSA 1972) (this excellent short guide to patrol leadership written for Scouts is still very useful even though it is a bit dated)

Phelps, *Resources for Leadership: Sourcebook for Managers of Learning* (2001), available at www.whitestag.org (this sourcebook provides an extremely comprehensive textbook treatment of Bela Banathy's "White Stag" youth leadership development program that was the basis for many decades of Wood Badge & BSA Junior Leadership Training).

The History of Wood Badge in the United States (BSA 1990)

For an impressive and comprehensive discussion of the first camp at Brownsea, see Colin "Johnny" Walker's wonderful web page at

http://www.Scouting.milestones.btinternet.co.uk/brownsea.htm

and his book on Brownsea: *B-P's Acorn, The World's First Scout Camp.*

For great games and traditional Scouting tips, see Rick Seymour's excellent website: www.inquiry.net

Troop Leadership Training (TLT)

The BSA expects Scoutmasters to conduct Troop Leadership Training. It can be challenging to develop an all-day or weekend program from the ground up. BSA publications for National Youth Leadership Training are excellent, but the BSA currently does not provide any turnkey solutions to busy Scoutmasters who want to conduct a full day or weekend of Troop Leadership Training and do not want to reinvent the wheel.

You can use the following Troop Leadership Training ideas as a model for a day or weekend training experience for your own troop. Through experience, we have found that self-discovery type games followed by reflections and seminars can be effective in building your troop leadership team. Keep lectures to a minimum. Listen and watch much more than you talk. Ask your Senior Patrol Leader to lead most of the activities and discussions.

Basic Troop Leadership Training Agenda

1. Opening Ceremony

2. Team Development (Forming, Storming, Norming, Performing)

3. Duties and Responsibilities of Patrol Leader

4. Teaching EDGE™

5. Leading EDGE™

6. Different Types of Leaders

7. What Makes a Good Leader?

8. Evaluation: Start, Stop & Continue (SCC) (Roses & Thorns)

9. Conflict Resolution

10. Basic Fundamentals on Planning: How to Plan, things to think about when planning

11. Monthly Program Planning

12. Weekly Meeting Agenda/Schedule Planning

13. Roses & Thorns About the Training Experience

14. Scoutmaster's Minute

Detailed Troop Leadership Training Weekend Model:

Participant Preparation: review BSA Senior Patrol Leader, Patrol Leader handbooks before training day. All Scouts and Scouter participants to dress in identical Scout shorts and Troop t-shirt uniforms.

Resources & Equipment (PLC to Bring from Home):

* Boy Scout Troop Leadership Training Book including leadership position handout cards

* blindfold material (each Scout should bring a neckerchief or bandanna)

* flip chart and marker (for the Scouts' use)

* Inflatable beach ball(s)

* notebook paper

* 40' rope

* "Sled" Equipment: two 12' 4x4s with 7 ropes of identical length fed through drilled holes spaced two inches apart

* Spider Web Escape: Twine, stakes or trees, small bells (Christmas tree ornament type), 10 - 12 short Bungee Cords

* "Plutonium Transportation" equipment: tin can, one thick rubber band, a number of thin rubber bands, twine cut into 6-foot lengths

* BSA "Trained" patches and certificates (to be awarded immediately following the training session)

I. Opening Ceremony: Purpose and Schedule

II. Warm-up Games: Forming the Team

1. *Leadership Game: Supporting Your Team* Leader stands in center, all participants join hands and form a circle wide enough so everyone feels some pull, then count off by two's. The "ones" lean forward, the "twos" lean backward.

2. *Leadership Game: Working Together* Scatter the group. Throw out a beach ball and ask the group to keep the beach ball up in the air as long as possible. The same person cannot hit the ball twice in succession. The team can compete against its own previous record.

III. Brief Introduction to Scout Leadership Themes

Senior Patrol Leader or Scoutmaster leads discussion about the overall training exercise and asks each participant what he hopes to take away from the day or weekend.

IV. Sharing Servant Leadership and Team Building (Leading EDGE™)

Leadership Game: Command Style of Leadership: All participants except Senior Patrol Leader form a line and put on their blindfolds. The 40-foot rope is handed to all participants. The participants must keep their hands on the rope and form a square under direction from the Senior Patrol Leader. No one except the Senior Patrol Leader may speak.

Reflection (conducted by Senior Patrol Leader)

* Who took a leadership role?

* How did decisions get made?

* What kind of leader did I portray?

* Did you like this style of leadership? If not, why not?

* How does it feel to be lead by a big boss?

* How often does "big boss" happen in Scouting?

* When is "big boss" style the right one?

* When is it the wrong one?

Leadership Game: "Paper Airplanes"

Phase I: Flying Solo Each person makes a paper airplane. The Senior Patrol Leader runs a contest to see whose airplane flies the furthest. The Scouts whose airplanes fly the furthest win the contest.

Phase II: Flying Wingtip to Wingtip The winners in Phase I teach the rest of the group how to make long-distance paper airplanes. The overall group is rated based on the average distance flown by all airplanes.

Reflection (conducted by Senior Patrol Leader):

* Who took leadership roles in Phase I? Was there any leadership?

* How did the leadership dynamic change in Phase II?

* Who was a teacher in Phase II? Is the teacher the same as the leader?

* Was the leader in Phase II someone whom you expected to become leader?

* How did the leaders feel in Phase II when they were suddenly being judged based on the combined performance of the group as a whole?

* What could the team have done to work better together in phase II?

Teambuilding Game: "Sled" The team needs to work together to "step" a pair of 4x4's across the field. Everyone must keep their feet on the two 4x4's at all times.

Reflection (conducted by Senior Patrol Leader):

* How did the group decide to solve the problem?

* How satisfied were you with how decisions were made?

* Who assumed leadership? Why?

* Did the leadership role shift? How did someone else gain leadership?

* Was leadership shared?

* How might this style of shared leadership work in our troop?

* Who made suggestions for how to complete the Objective?

* Why were some suggestions heard and others ignored?

* How did communication work in the game?

* What have you learned from this game?

* What did you learn about the others?

* If you were to do this exercise again, what would you do differently?

Teambuilding Game: "Plutonium Transportation" - The Senior Patrol Leader or his delegate produces the equipment: tin can, rubber bands, and twine. The team's mission: move plutonium (water) from one point to another without any spillage (even one spilled drop can contaminate the world with deadly radiation). The Scouts place the thick rubber band around the can. Each Scout receives a thin rubber band and a length of twine. The Scouts tie the thin rubber bands to the thick rubber band, maintaining even spacing around the circumference of the thick rubber band. The Scouts tie their length of twine to their thin rubber band. Water is placed into the can. The Scouts must work together to lift and transport the can without spilling its contents.

Reflection:

* How did the group work together?

* How satisfied were you with the leadership?

* Who assumed leadership? Why?

* What was the hardest part?

* How did communication work in the game?

Group Discussion: Identify traits of a good leader. Senior Patrol Leader lists the traits on a flip chart. Save the flip chart sheet as a memento of the weekend, and post it in your meeting room.

V. The Patrol Method

A. Group Nature Observation: The leader has the group count off by threes. All "ones" are Seers. Two's and Three's are hearers and feelers. The Hearers and Feelers put on blindfolds. Seers can say only what they see. Hearers can say only what they hear. Feelers can say only what they feel. The Leader and the Seers lead the Hearers and the Feelers on a (safe) nature course. The leader keeps a list of observations. The group gets a point for every item it collectively observes and lists.

Reflection

B. Facilitated Discussion:

The Patrol Method: what is it, why use it, how does it work? (see Sections 3 & 4)

VI. The Patrol Leaders Council, Troop Structure, Decisionmaking at the Lowest Level

Senior Patrol Leader Presentation: Troop Structure + Organizational Chart (from BSA Troop Leadership Training manual)

Forum: How does the Troop work? Is there a "chain of command" or does everyone answer to the Patrol Leaders Council? What positions do each of us hold? How do we work together?

Hand out cards from BSA Troop Leadership Training Guide

Discussion of how each Scout is important to the Troop and what his supporting role will be

Conduct an investiture ceremony

Reflection

VII. Team Building: Doing Your Best, Motivational Leadership, Recognition and Positive Reinforcement, Celebrating All Victories

Initiative Game: "Spider Web Escape" An Assistant Scoutmaster makes a "Spider Web" in advance from twine, stakes or trees, a small bell, and short bungee cords. The "Spider Web" consists of an irregular arrangement of ropes wrapped around two trees or two sets of closely spaced staves. A bell is suspended at the tension point of the ropes. The bungee cords are used to maintain tension throughout the web. Each touch of the ropes which rings the bell is a penalty. Each Scout must pass through a different hole to get through the web. The team must get everyone through the web. The event is timed, and can be repeated as teamwork improves.

VIII. Building Trust and Communication

Trustbuilding Game: Leading the Way All team members put on blindfolds. Two guides who will lead the blindfolded over an obstacle course are tapped and asked to remove their blindfolds. The guides remove their blindfolds and are shown the course. The guides can discuss communication strategies. The guides are not allowed to use language but can use sounds. Guides are not allowed to touch any member of the group.

Reflection

Trustbuilding Game: Trust Fall Each member of the team gets a chance to fall back into the arms of the rest of the team.

Reflection

IX. Leaving a Legacy of Leadership

Inspirational presentation and Scoutmaster's Minute, followed by team service project

"Don't try to do everything yourself or the boys will merely look on, and the scheme will flag."

— Robert Baden-Powell

Scout Oath

On my honor, I will do my best
To do my duty to God and my Country,
and to obey the Scout Law;
To help other people at all times;
To keep myself physically strong, mentally awake, and morally straight.

Scout Law

A Scout is Trustworthy, Loyal, Helpful, Friendly, Courteous, Kind,
Obedient, Cheerful, Thrifty, Brave, Clean and Reverent

Scout Motto

Be Prepared

Scout Slogan

Do a Good Turn Daily

Aims of Scouting

To build character: self-reliance, self-discipline, self-confidence and self-respect

To foster citizenship: love of community, country and world; commitment of service to others; and an understanding of democratic principles

To develop fitness: physical, emotional, and moral fitness that will stay with a Scout for the whole of his life

The Methods of Scouting

"A Game with a Purpose"

The Ideals (Oath, Law, Motto, Slogan)

The Patrol Method

The Outdoors

Advancement

Association with Adults

Personal Growth

Leadership Development

Uniform

William "Green Bar Bill" Hillcourt's "Ten Essentials of Scoutmastership" Reinterpreted

+ Believe in the boys

+ Focus on the boys' happiness through their formative years

+ Have faith in Scouting as THE program that will best mold our youth into fine men

+ Know that to the boys, Scouting is a game—to you, a game with a purpose

+ Know that to your boys, *you* are Scouting

+ Have focus and purpose to execute a planned program with energy, perseverance, patience and good humor

+ Be willing to submerge your ego. Give boy leaders the opportunity to lead and grow through the Patrol Method. Tell them The Why.

+ Get yourself fully trained

+ Work with other organizations for the good of the individual boy and the community

+ Love and cherish the outdoors

Difficulties in Working the Patrol Method

Excerpted from:

Capt. Roland E. Philipps, "The Patrol System"

(C. Arthur Pearson Ltd. Tower House London 1917)

It is possible that having read up to this point, a Scoutmaster may be thinking to himself, "I quite agree that the Patrol System is the best way in which a Troop can be organised and conducted, and am fully aware that many of the best Troops in the country are run entirely upon these lines, but in view of the exceptional circumstances in which I am placed it is quite impracticable to adopt Patrol Training in my own Troop." One Scoutmaster puts forward the peculiarity of his boys - their exceptional fickleness or their surprising solidity - another speaks of their scattered homes and of long distances to be traversed on dark winter nights. One Scoutmaster finds that in his Troop there are peculiar difficulties with regard to the older boys, while another discovers that he is singularly situated with regard to the younger ones. One man cannot work his Troop in Patrols because he has got no Assistant Scoutmaster, and another finds it impossible because he has a wife and three children and has to work late at the office.

The point to remember, however, is that there is no Troop, either in town or in country, which will not be all the better for working on the Founder's lines. Let it be at once admitted that there is hardly a Scoutmaster in the Brotherhood who is not an exceptional man working with extraordinary boys under unusual conditions with peculiar difficulties! That is the whole charm of it. The Movement itself is peculiar - peculiarly inspiring - and to make it a success one requires peculiarly helpful and original methods of training and organisation. Such methods are summed up under the heading - "The Patrol System." Again, a Scoutmaster may say, "I believe in this system of training, but I have run my Troop on other lines for two or three years and it is not possible now to make a change. If I could start again it would be different." May it, therefore, be stated here beyond any impossibility of ambiguity or misunderstanding that the Patrol System is no cut-and-dried plan, but arises from a special attitude of mind - a belief that the character training and education of a boy should be evolved from within rather than imposed from without. The boys, in fact, must make themselves into Scouts - nobody else can do it for them. The shirt and shorts may be imposed from without, but it is only out of the heart and mind of the boy himself that the Scouting spirit can be successfully evolved. This attitude of mind does not take years to produce. It comes within a week by re-reading "Scouting for Boys" from the boy's point of view.

The way to start the Patrol System is by having a preliminary talk with the boys about the idea of the Patrol as a self-contained unit, and then without any waste of time by establishing the Court of Honour [our Patrol Leaders Council] and the Patrol Competition as two permanent Troop institutions. The other developments will come by themselves.

Roland Philipps was killed in action in the Battle of the Somme on 7 July 1916 as he led his men to attack enemy trenches.

Acknowledgements

The authors thank the following people for their helpful contributions:

Phil Burr

Sharon Cunningham

J. Dvorsky

Héctor Escudero

Anne Faris

George Harkin

Chris Knight

Jesse Knight

Bob Mace

Gigi Toth

The Scouts of Troop 624

About the Authors & Illustrator

Rob Faris is a devoted husband and father of five. He loves camping, hiking, backpacking, campfire cooking, history, literature and music. His wife Anne "got" Scouting after reading an early draft of this book. His daughter has been a constant source of inspiration, enthusiasm and support. His oldest son Robert is an Eagle Scout. Other sons are active in Scouting and are following the Eagle trail.

Rob joined Boy Scout Troop 5 Brookfield Connecticut in 1969 on his 11th birthday. As a Scout, Rob camped consecutive months to earn the "Year Round Camper Award" seven years in a row. Rob served in all Troop leadership positions including Den Chief, Patrol Leader, Senior Patrol Leader and JASM. He attended Junior Leadership Training, participated with his Troop in 1973 National Jamboree East, and earned his Eagle award. When his oldest son Robert turned 11 years old, Rob again put on the uniform and became active in Scouting on the Troop and district levels. Wood Badge changed Rob's life. Since earning his beads, Rob's passion has been to inspire personal responsibility, self-reliance, good citizenship and ethical conduct in youth through application of the Patrol Method. A 2009 Philmont Trek convinced him that all Scouts should go to Philmont.

Rob received his law degree *summa cum laude* from Notre Dame Law School. He serves on the management team of a mid-sized Arlington Virginia intellectual property law firm he co-founded.

Ted Knight is a management consultant specializing in health service planning, business planning, economic development and program design for small communities. He routinely conducts a wide variety of training seminars and workshops for community and corporate leaders.

Scouting has always been a big part of Ted's life. He has been active as a Scout leader most of his adult life, since 1965.

Ted began in Scouting as a Cub Scout in Pack 106 Arlington Virginia in 1955. Ted joined Boy Scouts in Troop 106 and served as Patrol Leader, Senior Patrol Leader, Junior Assistant Scoutmaster and Order of the Arrow Chapter Chief. He joined Post 106 in 1962. He attended Junior Leader Training in 1961 and earned his Eagle Award in 1962.

Ted completed his BSA Wood Badge adult leadership training (Bear Patrol) in 1991. His objectives in Scouting are to teach the history, traditions and principles of Scouting as envisioned by Lord Baden-Powell of Gilwell and to work with those Scouts who are truly interested in achieving the rank of Eagle Scout. He has been associated with several Boy Scout and Venturing units.

Ted is an avid outdoorsman and hunter. He is married and the proud father of three grown children and grandfather of three. He has written other books on personal, business and organizational management.

He earned a Master's Degree in Hospital Administration from The Medical College of Virginia and a Bachelor's Degree in History from George Mason College of the University of Virginia.

Harry Wimbrough joined Scouting with Troop 24 in Wellsboro, Pennsylvania in 1969. As a Scout, Harry served in all Scout leadership positions within the Troop. Harry earned his Eagle Award in 1975 and was active in the Order of the Arrow.

Harry enlisted in the United States Army in 1975. Over the years, he served in numerous leadership positions from team leader to Command Sergeant Major (CSM) in a number of infantry units. Harry is a combat veteran, having participated in the Airborne Assault of Panama with the 75th Ranger Regiment during operation Just Cause. He retired from the U.S. Army in 2005 as a Command Sergeant Major of the 3rd United States Infantry Regiment, The Old Guard (the Army's official ceremonial unit and escort to the President) after 30 years of service to our nation.

Harry is a graduate of the Non-Commissioned Officer Basic, Advanced, Sergeants Major and Command Sergeants Major leadership courses. He is also a graduate of the Ranger, Airborne, Jumpmaster, Jungle Warfare, Winter Warfare Instructor, Air Movement and Hazardous Cargo Operations, Battle Staff and Garrison Command Sergeants Major courses. Harry received numerous awards and decorations while in the U.S. Army including Legion of Merit with Oak Leaf Cluster, Ranger Tab and Expert Infantryman's Badge. Harry was inducted into the Order of Saint Maurice and is a Distinguished Member of the 3rd Infantry Regiment. As Command Sergeant Major of the Old Guard, he took part in both the State Funeral of President Ronald Reagan and the Inauguration of President George W. Bush.

Harry likes to camp, cook, hike, scuba dive and hunt. He was married in 1983. He completed Wood Badge for the 21st Century leadership training in 2009. His son Joe has completed National Youth Leadership Training and is on the Eagle trail.

About the Illustrator

Joseph Durel earned his Eagle Scout award in 2008. He has served as Patrol Leader and Senior Patrol Leader of Troop 624 Arlington Virginia. He is enthusiastic about Baden-Powell's writings and drawings. He has been drawing from an early age, but only seriously since the seventh grade. His artistic interests range from mostly fantasy characters to graphic art. His gallery can be found at jadematrix.deviantart.com.

The authors and the illustrator are currently associated with Troop 624, Chain Bridge District, National Capital Area Council serving Northern Virginia, Washington D.C. and Southern Maryland.

Photograph and Illustration Credits

To order additional copies of
this book, visit our website:

http://www.Scoutleadership.com

Notes

BOBWHITE BLATHER - BLOG